2C

2 FEB

3 J

17

GW00707708

Charles Dickens's
Hard Times

Adapted for the stage by
Stephen Jeffreys

Samuel French – London
New York – Sydney – Toronto – Hollywood

© 1987 BY STEPHEN JEFFREYS

1. This play is fully protected under the Copyright Laws of the British Commonwealth of Nations, the United States of America and all countries of the Berne and Universal Copyright Conventions.

2. All rights, including Stage, Motion Picture, Radio, Television, Public Reading, and Translation into Foreign Languages, are strictly reserved.

---

3. **No part of this publication may lawfully be reproduced in ANY form or by any means—photocopying, typescript, recording (including video-recording), manuscript, electronic, mechanical, or otherwise—or be transmitted or stored in a retrieval system, without prior permission.**

---

4. Rights of Performance by Amateurs are controlled by SAMUEL FRENCH LTD, 52 FITZROY STREET, LONDON W1P 6JR, and they, or their authorized agents, issue licences to amateurs on payment of a fee. **It is an infringement of the Copyright to give any performance or public reading of the play before the fee has been paid and the licence issued.**

5. Licences are issued subject to the understanding that it shall be made clear in all advertising matter that the audience will witness an amateur performance; that the names of the authors of the plays shall be included on all announcements and on all programmes; and that the integrity of the author's work will be preserved.

    The Royalty Fee indicated below is subject to contract and subject to variation at the sole discretion of Samuel French Ltd.

    > Basic fee for each and every
    > performance by amateurs   Code M
    > in the British Isles

    In Theatres or Halls seating Six Hundred or more the fee will be subject to negotiation.

    In Territories Overseas the fee quoted above may not apply. A fee will be quoted on application to our local authorized agent, or if there is no such agent, on application to Samuel French Ltd, London.

6. The Professional Rights in this play are controlled by Margaret Ramsay Ltd, 14a Goodwin's Court, St Martin's Lane, London WC2

ESSEX COUNTY LIBRARY

The publication of this play does not imply that it is necessarily available for performance by amateurs or professionals, either in the British Isles or Overseas. Amateurs and professionals considering a production are strongly advised in their own interests to apply to the appropriate agents for consent before starting rehearsals or booking a theatre or hall.

ISBN 0 573 01659 3

HARD TIMES

This adaptation was first performed on June 16th 1982 at the Brewery Arts Centre, Kendal, by Pocket Theatre, Cumbria, with the following cast:

Gradgrind, Tom,   Philip George
Blackpool, Waiter

Bounderby, Sleary, Bitzer,   Steve Tomlin
Harthouse, Slackbridge

Louisa, Emma Gordon,
Mrs Blackpool, Mrs Pegler,   Madeleine Hateley
Chairwoman

Sissy, Mrs Gradgrind,
Mrs Sparsit, Rachael,   Christine Woodcock
Mary Stokes

The play was directed by Adrian Harris
Designed by Anthony Clement

The first London performance of *Hard Times* was given at the Orange Tree Theatre, Richmond, directed by Sam Waters. The parts were doubled as above, and played by Frank Moorey, David Timson, Kate Spiro and Caroline John.

The play is set in Coketown, an industrial town in Lancashire, in the 1840s.

PRODUCTION NOTE

If a company of four is used the doubling given on page iii is the only possible casting.

If more actors are available the play could be cast quite differently, but all the performers should take a roughly equal role, those carrying fewer characters bearing more of the narrative.

Hard Times can be played either with an interval after Scene 19, or with two intervals—one at the end of Book One and the other at the end of Book Two.

CHARACTERS

Mr Gradgrind, proprietor of the model school, later
  MP
Sissy Jupe, a stroller's daughter
Bitzer, a pupil, later light porter at the bank
Louisa, Gradgrind's daughter
Josiah Bounderby, a self-made man, friend to
  Gradgrind
Mrs Gradgrind, Gradgrind's wife
Mr Sleary, proprietor of Sleary's Horse-Riding
Emma Gordon, a performer in the above
Mrs Sparsit, keeper of Bounderby's house
Tom, Gradgrind's son
Stephen Blackpool, a weaver
Rachael, a weaver
Mrs Blackpool, Stephen's wife
Mrs Pegler, an old woman from the country
James Harthouse, a young man of means
Slackbridge, a Trade Union delegate
Mary Stokes, a weaver
Chairwoman
Waiter
Hands, wedding guests, station officials, rescuers etc.

INTRODUCTION

This adaptation of *Hard Times* was commissioned by Pocket Theatre Cumbria for a company of four. The original production and the subsequent revivals called for each actor to portray a number of roles as well as taking a share of the passages of direct narration. Audiences have generally enjoyed this approach enormously; in addition to a close encounter with Dickens's genius, they have been able to sit back and watch four people working extremely hard for over three hours, changing costumes and characters at top speed, delivering lengthy sections of classic prose and conjuring up the whole range of human emotion. This four-actor version has been reproduced here, but I must stress that other approaches to the text are possible and, in many cases will be desirable.

Professional companies who can afford a fifth or sixth actor to spread the workload would be able to do so without losing the excitement generated by a small cast. Amateur companies might consider using a company of say, between eight and twelve, giving each actor a couple of parts and a share of the narration. This approach would retain the idea of doubling roles without stretching performers beyond their limits. Schools or larger amateur groups could cast each role individually, perhaps even utilizing a group of narrators to speak the passages of direct address. Directors of larger scale productions should also take the opportunities afforded for "crowd" scenes: the entry of Sleary's Horse-Riding, the first appearance of the Hands, the Union Meeting, the rescue from the Old Hell Shaft could all benefit from the availability of extras

Hard Times is quite a long play. In order to sustain the momentum of the story, it is necessary to keep the action moving continuously, so designers should aim for simplicity and speed, only using props and furniture which can be quickly removed by the actors.

I have tried to be as faithful to Dickens's novel as possible. Some changes have been occasioned by the necessity of keeping characters played by the same actor away from each other. The only major liberty I have taken occurs in the Union Meeting scene where, in the novel, Stephen Blackpool refuses to join the Union because of an obscure promise he has made. Most readers of the novel are baffled by the inadequate explanation Blackpool gives for his behaviour, and commentators of all persuasions have identified this moment as the weak link in the narrative's chain. Blackpool is temperamentally an outsider in an explosive political situation, so I felt he should refuse to join the Union because he doesn't believe in Unions. For me this alteration transforms the Union Meeting scene into a political debate and makes Stephen Blackpool's fate tragic—he is conscious of the choice he makes, acts upon it and suffers the consequences.

My thanks are due to Adrian Harris who commissioned the play and the cast who first brought it triumphantly to life; to Sam Waters and the company at the Orange Tree who revived it so splendidly, and to my father Jack Jeffreys who loved Dickens.

Stephen Jeffreys

Prologue

A bare stage

Five minutes or so before the show goes up, the actors come on and chat with the audience. Then the following is sung to signal the beginning of the play.

(See p. 78 for music)

Solo Good people all, both great and small,
Come listen to my rhymes;
I'll sing to you a verse or two
Concerning of the times:
All The Cotton Lords of Lancashire
Are plucking up their feathers;
They are a mob, so help me Bob,
Of humbugs altogether.

There never was such hard times seen in England before.

The following is then spoken as a chorus:

Actor 1 Coketown.
Actress 1 A triumph of fact.
Actor 2 Coketown.
Actress 2 A place devoid of fancy.
Actor 1 Coketown.
Actress 1 A town of brick that would have been red if the smoke and ashes had allowed it.
Actor 2 Coketown.
Actress 2 A town of unnatural red and black like the face of a painted savage.
Actor 1 A town of machinery and tall chimneys, out of which interminable serpents of smoke trailed themselves for ever and ever and never got uncoiled.
Actress 1 A town with a black canal and a river that ran purple with ill-smelling dye.
Actor 2 Vast piles of buildings full of windows where there was a rattling and a trembling all day long ...
Actress 2 And where the piston of the steam-engine worked monotonously up and down like the head of an elephant in a state of melancholy madness.
Actor 1 A town inhabited by children all very like one another ...
Actress 1 Parts of the Coketown machine ...
Actor 2 Stripped of all fancy ...
Actress 2 Shaped on the anvil of fact ...
Actor 1 Worked in the furnace of fact ...

Actress 1 Turned out in that great factory of fact . . .
Actor 2 Mr Gradgrind's model school.
Actress 1 *Hard Times* by Charles Dickens. Book the First: "Sowing".

SCENE 1

The Lights come up on a schoolroom. Children are sitting in rows on wooden benches. Thomas Gradgrind stands, addressing them

Gradgrind Now, what I want is, Facts. Facts alone are wanted in life. Plant nothing else in your mind and root out everything else. The minds of reasoning animals must be formed on Facts: nothing else will be of any service to them. This is the principle on which I bring up my own children, and this is the principle on which the children in this school will be brought up. So you will stick to Facts. (*Out front*) Thomas Gradgrind, sir. A man of realities. A man of fact and calculations. A man who proceeds on the principle that two and two are four, and nothing over, and who is not to be talked into allowing for anything over. Thomas Gradgrind, sir, with a rule and a pair of scales, and the multiplication table always in his pocket, sir, ready to weigh and measure any parcel of human nature and tell you exactly what it comes to. It is a mere question of figures, a case of simple arithmetic. (*He points at Sissy*) I don't know that girl. Girl number twenty. Who is that girl?
Sissy (*standing, curtsying*) Sissy Jupe, sir.
Gradgrind Sissy is not a name. Call yourself Cecilia.
Sissy It's Father as calls me Sissy sir.
Gradgrind Then he has no business to do it. What is your father?
Sissy He belongs to the Horse-Riding if you please, sir.
Gradgrind We don't want to know anything about that here. Your father breaks horses doesn't he?
Sissy If you please, sir, when they can get any to break, they do break horses in the ring, sir.
Gradgrind Very well then, describe your father as a horsebreaker. He doctors sick horses I daresay?
Sissy Oh yes, sir.
Gradgrind Very well then, he is a veterinary surgeon, a farrier and a horse-breaker. Give me your definition of a horse.
Sissy I . . . er . . . I don't . . .

Pause

Gradgrind Girl number twenty unable to define a horse. Girl number twenty possessed of no facts in reference to one of the commonest of animals! Some boy's definition of a horse. Bitzer, yours.

Bitzer stands

Bitzer Quadruped. Graminivorous. Forty teeth, namely twenty-four grinders, four eye-teeth and twelve incisive. Sheds coat in the spring; in marshy countries sheds hoofs too. Hoofs hard, but requiring to be shod with iron. Age known by marks in mouth. Sir. (*He knuckles his forehead and sits down*)

Gradgrind Now girl number twenty. You know what a horse is.

Sissy sits down

Very well. That's a horse. Now let me ask you, girls and boys: would you
paper a room with representations of horses?

*The class say "Yes, sir", then, seeing Gradgrind's reaction, change to "No,
sir"*

Of course, no. Why wouldn't you?

Dead silence

All right then, I'll explain to you. Do you ever see horses walking up and
down the sides of rooms in reality—in fact? Do you? Of course not. Why
then, you are not to see anywhere what you don't see in fact: you are not
to have anywhere what you don't have in fact. What is called Taste is only
another name for Fact. This is a new principle, a discovery, a great
discovery. Now I'll try you again. Suppose you were going to carpet a
room. Would you use a carpet having representations of flowers upon it?

A general chorus of "No, sir" apart from Sissy who says "Yes, sir"

Girl number twenty.

Sissy stands

You would carpet a room with representations of flowers. Why?
Sissy If you please, sir, I am very fond of flowers.
Gradgrind So you would have people walking over them in heavy boots?
Sissy It wouldn't hurt them, sir. They would just be pictures of what is
pretty and I fancy——
Gradgrind Ay, ay, ay! But you mustn't fancy. That's it. You are never to
fancy. Fact, fact, fact. That's what I want. Fact, fact, fact.

The pupils disperse

The Lights concentrate around Gradgrind

SCENE 2

Gradgrind Mr Gradgrind walked homeward from the school in a state of
considerable satisfaction. It was his school, and he intended it to be a
model. He intended every child in it to be a model—just as the young
Gradgrinds were models. There were two young Gradgrinds, and they
had been lectured at from their tenderest years: coursed like little hares.
To his matter-of-fact home, which was called Stone Lodge, Mr Gradgrind directed his steps. He had virtually retired from the wholesale
hardware trade before he built Stone Lodge, and was now looking about
for a suitable opportunity of making an arithmetical figure in parliament.
Stone Lodge was situated on a moor within a mile or two of a great
town—Coketown. He had reached the neutral ground upon the outskirts
of the town when his ears were invaded by the sound of music.

The Company create Sleary's Horse-Riding Circus, utilizing whatever skills are available. The effect should be to create as dramatic a contrast as possible with the schoolroom scene. Perhaps the following speech is interpreted visually

Sleary Roll up, roll up for Thleary'th Horthe-Riding. Inaugurating the entertainment, Mith Jothephine Thleary will perform her gratheful equethtrian Tyrolean flower act. Then, in an act that mutht be theen to be believed, Thignor Jupe will eluthidate the diverting accomplithmenth of hith highly-trained performing dog, Merrylegth. Thignor Jupe will then exhibit hith athtounding feat of throwing theventy-five hundredweight in rapid thuccethion back-handed over hith head, thuth forming a fountain of tholid iron in mid-air, a feat never before attemped in thith, or any other country, the performanthe being enlivened by a volley of chathte Thakethpearian quipth and retorth.

The circus dissolves and is replaced by a group of children, including Louisa. They are clustered together as if peering through a hole in the circus tent

Gradgrind Thomas Gradgrind took no heed of these trivialities of course, but passed on as a practical man ought to pass on. But the turning of the road took him by the back of the booth, and at the back of the booth, a number of children were congregated in a number of stealthy attitudes, striving to peep in at the hidden glories of the place. Among them, to his amazement, whom did he then behold, but his own daughter, Louisa.

Gradgrind comes upon the children

Louisa!!

The other children run away

In the name of wonder, idleness and folly, what do you do here?
Louisa Wanted to see what it was like.
Gradgrind What it was like?
Louisa Yes, Father.
Gradgrind You Louisa, to whom the circle of the sciences is open; you who may be said to be replete with facts; you who have been trained to mathematical exactness; you here in this degraded position! I am amazed!
Louisa I was tired. I have been tired a long time.
Gradgrind Tired? Of what?
Louisa I don't know of what. Of everything I think.
Gradgrind Say not another word. I will hear no more. What would your best friends say, Louisa? Do you attach no value to their good opinion? What would Mr Bounderby say?

Pause

What would Mr Bounderby say?

He leads her off

The Lights cross-fade, picking out Actor 1

SCENE 3

Actor 1 Who *was* Mr Bounderby? He was a rich man: banker, merchant, manufacturer and what not. A big loud man with a stare and a metallic laugh. A man who was the bully of humility, and as near to being Mr Gradgrind's bosom friend as a man perfectly devoid of sentiment could be to another man perfectly devoid of sentiment. In the formal drawing-room of Stone Lodge, standing on the hearth rug, warming himself before the fire, Mr Bounderby delivered some observations to Mrs Gradgrind on the circumstance of its being his birthday.

Actor 1 instantly becomes Bounderby standing in the plainly furnished drawing-room of Stone Lodge. Mrs Gradgrind, "a little, thin, white, pink-eyed bundle of shawls" is sitting at her needlework

Bounderby I hadn't a shoe to my foot. As to a stocking, I didn't know such a thing by name. I spent the day in a ditch and the night in a pigsty. That's the way I spent my tenth birthday. Not that a ditch was new to me, for I was born in a ditch.

Mrs Gradgrind I do hope it was a dry ditch, Mr Bounderby.

Bounderby No! As wet as a sop. A foot of water in it.

Mrs Gradgrind Enough to give a baby a cold.

Bounderby Cold? I was born with inflammation of the lungs, and of everything else that was capable of inflammation. For years I was one of the most miserable little wretches ever seen. How I fought through it I don't know. I was determined I suppose. Here I am Mrs Gradgrind, anyhow, and nobody to thank for being here but myself.

Mrs Gradgrind Well, I only hope that your mother looked after——

Bounderby My mother? Bolted, ma'am.

Mrs Gradgrind Oh.

Bounderby My mother left me to my grandmother, and, according to my remembrance, she was the wickedest old woman who ever lived. She sold my one pair of shoes for drink. Why, I have known that grandmother of mine take her fourteen glasses of liquor in bed before breakfast.

Mrs Gradgrind Dear, dear.

Bounderby She kept a chandler's shop and kept me in an egg box. As soon as I was big enough, I ran away. Then I became a young vagabond; and instead of one old woman knocking me about and starving me, everybody of all ages knocked me about and starved me. I was a nuisance, an encumbrance and a pest. But I pulled through. Vagabond, errand-boy, vagabond, labourer, porter, clerk, chief manager, small partner, Josiah Bounderby of Coketown. That was my education. Tell Josiah Bounderby of Coketown of your district schools and your model schools and your training schools and your whole kettle-of-fish schools; and Josiah Bounderby tells you plainly, all right, all correct—he hadn't such advantages, the education that made him won't do for everybody, and you may force him to swallow boiling fat, but you shall never force him to suppress the facts of his life.

Gradgrind comes in with Louisa

Gradgrind Ah, Bounderby.

Bounderby Well, Gradgrind. And what is young Louisa in the dumps about?

Louisa Father caught me peeping at the circus.

All disapprove mightily

Mrs Gradgrind What can you possibly want to know of circuses? I am sure you have enough to do as it is. With my head in its present state, I couldn't remember the mere names of half the facts you have to attend to.

Louisa That's the reason.

Mrs Gradgrind Don't tell me that's the reason, because it can be nothing of the sort. Go and be somethingological directly.

Louisa goes

Mrs Gradgrind subsides

Gradgrind Bounderby, you are always so interested in my young people, particularly Louisa, that I make no apology for saying to you that I am very much vexed by this discovery. I have systematically devoted myself to the education of the reason of my family. The reason is the only faculty to which education should be addressed. And yet, Bounderby, it would appear from the circumstances of today as if something had crept into Louisa's mind which has never been intended to be developed, and in which reason has no part. In what has this vulgar curiosity its rise?

Bounderby I'll tell you what. In idle imagination.

Gradgrind I hope not. I confess however that the misgiving *has* crossed my mind on the way home.

Bounderby In idle imagination, Gradgrind, a very bad thing for anybody, but a cursed bad thing for a girl like Louisa.

Gradgrind In minds that have been practically formed by rule and line from the cradle upwards, this is so curious, so incomprehensible.

Bounderby Stop a bit. You have one of those strollers' children in the school.

Gradgrind Cecilia Jupe by name.

Bounderby Now stop a bit. How did she come there?

Gradgrind She especially applied, here at the house, to be admitted, as not regularly belonging to our town, and—yes, you are right, Bounderby, you are right. Louisa would have seen her then—though in Mrs Gradgrind's presence of course.

Bounderby Pray, Mrs Gradgrind, what passed?

Mrs Gradgrind Oh my poor health. The girl wanted to come to the school, and Mr Gradgrind wanted girls to come to the school, and Louisa said the girl wanted to come and Mr Gradgrind wanted girls to come, and how was it possible to contradict them when such was the fact.

Intimidated, she scuttles off

Bounderby Now I tell you what, Gradgrind. Turn the girl to the rightabout and there's an end to it.

Gradgrind I am much of your opinion. I have the father's address.

Bounderby Well then, Gradgrind. You know my motto. Do it at once.

Gradgrind If you will excuse me, Bounderby, I will accede to your suggestion and take up the business on the instant.

Bounderby Do it at once.

Gradgrind I'll walk back to town this moment.

Bounderby If you don't object to the suggestion, might I perhaps have a word with your daughter on the subject.

Gradgrind By all means, Bounderby. I'll have her shown in.

Gradgrind goes

Bounderby warms himself at the fire

Bounderby Circuses!

Louisa comes in

It's all right now, Louisa. You won't do such wrong any more. I'll answer for it being all over with your father. (*He pauses*) Well, Louisa? That's worth a kiss, isn't it?

Pause

Louisa You can take one, Mr Bounderby.

Slowly, she walks towards him, turns her cheek to him. He kisses her

Bounderby Always my pet, an't you Louisa?

She is still. Pause

Goodbye, Louisa.

Bounderby goes

Louisa rubs the spot he has kissed with her handkerchief

The Lights cross-fade to Gradgrind

SCENE 4

A bare stage

Gradgrind To that part of Coketown known as Pod's End, Mr Gradgrind walked, attaining at last the dubious refuge of a public house known as the *Pegasus's Arms*, where, according to his best information, Jupe and her father were numbered among the inhabitants. After calling out for some time, Mr Gradgrind found himself face to face with a stout man who seemed not quite sober and not quite drunk.

Sleary comes on. He has "one fixed eye and one loose eye" and wears a top hat with a brightly-coloured ribbon tied around it

Sleary Thquire. My name'th Thleary, proprietor of Thleary'th Horthe-Riding. Your thervant.

Gradgrind My name is Thomas Gradgrind, proprietor of the model school. I have come to see Mr Jupe, father to Cecilia.

Sleary Well, Thquire. Thith ith a matter that may prethent some difficulty. You may or may not be aware (for perhapth you have not been much in the audienth) that Jupe hath very often mithed hith tip lately.

Gradgrind Has—what has he missed?

Sleary Mithed his tip, Thquire. Offered at the garterth four timeth latht night and never thurmounted them. Mithed hith tip at the bannerth too, and was loothe in his ponging.

Gradgrind Loose in his ponging? I beg your pardon, Mr Sleary, but I am unable to catch the meaning of all this.

Sleary I mean, Thquire, that he didn't do what he ought to hath done. He was thort in hith leapth and bad in hith tumbling.

Gradgrind Ah.

Sleary That, in a general way, ith mithing hith tip.

Gradgrind I see sir. Be that as it may, the sole reason for my presence here is to deliver a message of some importance to this same Jupe.

Sleary Then my opinion, Thquire, ith that he will never rethieve it. Do you know much of him?

Gradgrind I never saw the man in my life.

Sleary Then I doubt if you ever *will* thee him now. He and hith dog are thuppothed to have morrithed. (*He pauses*) Gone off.

Gradgrind Do you mean that he has deserted his daughter? This is devilish good. What were the circumstances of his departure?

Sleary He thent hith daughter out on an errand not an hour ago, to buy a bottle of nine oilth—thath for hith bruitheth—and hathn't been theen thince. Thethilia cannot believe it of him, but he hath cut away and left her.

Gradgrind Pray, why can she not believe it of him?

Sleary Becauth thothe two were ath one. Becauth they were never ath-under. Becauth up to thith time, he theemed to dote on her. She ith thearching the thtreeth for him at thith moment. Poor Thithy! If you should happen to hath looked in tonight for the purpoth of telling him that you were going to do her any little thervith, it would be very fortunate and well-timed.

Gradgrind On the contrary, I came to tell him that her connections made her not an object for the school. Still, if her father really has left her, without any connivance on her part, that alters the complexion of things.

During this last, Emma Gordon has come on. She is colourfully but poorly dressed and behaves with maternal devotion to Sissy

Emma Pardon me, sir, d'you mean you're going to be able to do something for our poor Sissy?

Sleary Emma Gordon, Thquire, tight-rope walker.

Gradgrind Thomas Gradgrind, ma'am. Perhaps so. I must put something directly to her. But here comes the girl now.

Sissy runs on, distraught. She carries a bottle of oil

Sissy Is Father not here? Then he must have gone! He's left me!

She runs to Emma who comforts her

Sleary Ith an eternal thame, upon my thoul it ith.

Sissy Father! You are gone to try to do me some good, I know. But how will you be able to live without me?

Emma He'll be back my love. He won't have forgotten you.

Sissy He must come back, he must come back.

Gradgrind Well, whether or not this person is to be expected back at any time is of no moment. He is gone away and there is no present expectation of his return. That I believe is agreed on all hands.

Sleary Thath agreed, Thquire.

Gradgrind Well then, I, who came here to inform Jupe's father that she could no longer be received at the school, am prepared in these altered circumstances to make a proposal. I am willing to take charge of you, Jupe, and to educate you and provide for you. The only condition I make is that you decide now, at once whether to accompany me or to remain here. Also, that if you accompany me now, it is understood that you communicate no more with any of your friends who are here present. These observations comprise the whole of the case.

Sleary At the same time, I muth put in my word, Thquire, tho that both thideth of the banner may be equally theen. If you like, Thethilia to be prentith, you know the nature of the work and you know your companionth, tho you'll be very welcome. I never wath much of a cackler, Thquire, and I have thaid my thay.

Gradgrind The only observation I will make to you, Jupe, in the way of influencing your decision, is that a sound practical education is highly desirable, and that even your father himself appears to have known and felt that much.

Sissy stops crying and looks at Gradgrind

Be sure you know your own mind, Jupe, I say no more. Be sure you know your own mind.

Sissy When Father comes back, how will he ever find me if I go away?

Gradgrind You may be quite at ease on that score. In such a case, your father must find out Mr Sleary who would then let him know where you went. He would have no difficulty at any time in finding Thomas Gradgrind of Coketown. I am well known.

A pause. Sissy's decision

Sissy Give me my clothes. Give me my clothes and let me go away before I break my heart.

Emma goes off

Gradgrind You are quite determined, Jupe?

Sissy I am, sir.

Gradgrind Then take your farewell of these people and come with me.

Sissy goes to Sleary who opens his arms wide and takes her hands

Sleary Goodbye, my dear! You'll make your fortune, I hope, and none of our poor folkth will ever trouble you, I pound it. (*He kisses her*)

Emma comes back with the bundle of clothes. She hugs Sissy

Emma Goodbye, Sissy my love, come and see us when you're a lady.

Sleary There the ith, Thquire and the'll do you juthtithe. Goodbye, Thethilia!

Sissy Goodbye.

Sleary Leave the nine oilth, my dear, it will be of no uthe to you now.
Sissy No. Let me keep it for Father till he comes back. He had no thought
of going away when he sent me for it. I must keep it for him!
Sleary Tho be it, dear.

Sleary and Emma at one side of the stage, Gradgrind and Sissy at the other

Farewell. Thtick to the termth of your engagement, be obedient to the
Thquire and forget uth. But if you're ever grown up and well-off, and you
come upon any horth-riding, don't be hard on it. Give it a bethpeak, and
think you might do worth. People mutht be amuthed. They can't alwayth
be a-learning. Make the betht of uth, not the wurtht. I lay down the whole
philothophy of horth-riding when I say to you: "Make the betht of uth,
not the wurtht."

Sleary and Emma wave them goodbye

Immediately Actress 1 returns

SCENE 5

Actress 1 Mr Bounderby being a bachelor, an elderly lady presided over his
establishment in consideration of an annual stipend. Mrs Sparsit was the
lady's name; and she was a prominent figure in attendance on Mr
Bounderby's car as it rolled along in triumph with the bully of humility
inside. For Mrs Sparsit had not only seen different days, but was highly
connected. She had a great aunt living in these very times called Lady
Scadgers. Lady Scadgers, an immensely fat old woman, contrived the
marriage when Sparsit was just of age. Thus, when he died at twenty-four
(the scene of his decease Calais, the cause brandy), he did not leave his
widow, from whom he had been separated soon after the honeymoon, in
affluent circumstances. That bereaved lady, Mrs Sparsit, fifteen years
older than he, fell presently at deadly feud with her only relative, Lady
Scadgers; and, partly to spite her ladyship, and partly to maintain herself,
went out at a salary. (*She starts to become Mrs Sparsit*) And here she was
now, in her elderly days, with the Coriolanian style of nose and the dense
black eyebrows which had captivated Sparsit, making Mr Bounderby's
tea as he took his breakfast.

She takes her seat opposite Bounderby at the breakfast table

Mrs Sparsit Mr Bounderby, you are unusually slow, sir, with your breakfast this morning.
Bounderby Why, ma'am, I'm thinking about Tom Gradgrind's whim of
bringing up the tumbling girl.
Mrs Sparsit The girl is now waiting to know whether she is to go straight to
the school or up to the lodge.
Bounderby She must wait, ma'am, till I know myself. We shall have Tom
Gradgrind here presently, I suppose. If he should wish her to remain here
a day or two longer, of course she can, ma'am. I told him I would give her
a shake-down here last night in order that he might sleep on it before he
decided to let her have any association with Louisa.

Mrs Sparsit It was very thoughtful of you, sir.

They drink tea

Bounderby It's tolerably clear to *me*, that the little puss can get small good out of such companionship.

Pause

Mrs Sparsit Are you speaking of Miss Gradgrind, Mr Bounderby?

Bounderby Yes, ma'am, I am speaking of Louisa.

Mrs Sparsit Your observation being limited to "little puss", and there being two girls in question, I did not know which might be indicated by the expression.

Bounderby Louisa.

Mrs Sparsit Ah.

Bounderby Louisa. (*He pauses*) Louisa.

Mrs Sparsit You are quite another father to Louisa, sir.

Bounderby If you had said I was another father to young Tom, you might have been nearer the mark. I am going to take young Tom into my office. Under my wing, you might say, ma'am.

Mrs Sparsit Indeed? Rather young for that is he not?

Bounderby I am not taking him in at once. He is to finish his cramming first. By the Lord Harry, he'd open his eyes, that boy would, if he knew how empty of learning my young maw was at his time of life.

Mrs Sparsit Quite so, sir.

Bounderby But it's extraordinary, the difficulty I have in speaking on equal terms with people on scores of subjects. I have been speaking to you this morning about tumblers. Why, what do *you* know about tumblers? At the time when to have been a tumbler on the streets would have been a godsend to me, a prize in the lottery, you were coming out of the Italian Opera in white satin and jewels.

Mrs Sparsit I certainly was familiar with the Italian Opera at a very early age, sir.

Bounderby Egad, ma'am, so was I. A hard bed the pavement of its arcade used to make, I assure you. People like you, ma'am, accustomed since infancy to lie on down feathers have no idea how *hard* a paving stone is.

Mrs Sparsit Quite so, sir.

Bounderby After all, you must confess that you were born in the lap of luxury yourself. Come, ma'am, you know you were born in the lap of luxury.

Mrs Sparsit I do not deny it, sir.

Bounderby And you were in crack society, devilish high society.

Mrs Sparsit It is true, sir.

Bounderby You were in the tip-top fashion and all the rest of it.

Mrs Sparsit Yes sir, it is unquestionably true.

Gradgrind comes on. He gives a formal, prepared statement, pre-empting Bounderby's disapproval of his scheme

Gradgrind I have decided, Bounderby, to take the girl Jupe into my house. When she is not in attendance at the school, she can find employment about Mrs Gradgrind. I have explained to Louisa the miserable but natural end to her late career, and will impress upon Jupe that the whole of the subject is past and not to be referred to any more. I shall have the satisfaction of giving her a strict education; and she will be a living proof of the advantages of the training she will receive. She will be reclaimed and formed. Now then, Bounderby, what do you think of that?

Bounderby In your shoes, I shouldn't do as you are doing. But very well, very well. Since you are bent upon it, very well.

Gradgrind (*out front*) So Mr Gradgrind took Cecilia Jupe off with him to Stone Lodge.

He goes

Bounderby And Mr Bounderby went about his daily pursuits.

He goes

Mrs Sparsit (*slowly, with a suggestion of insight*) And Mrs Sparsit got behind her eyebrows and meditated in the gloom of that retreat all evening.

The Lights fade around Mrs Sparsit

Immediately Actor 2, Actress 2 come on, setting up the chairs for the next scene as they speak

SCENE 6

Actress 2 When she was half a dozen years younger, Louisa had begun a conversation with her brother one day by saying, "Tom, I wonder . . ."

Actor 2 Upon which Mr Gradgrind, overhearing, stepped forth into the light and said "Louisa, never wonder".

Actress 2 Herein lay the spring of the mechanical art and mystery of educating the reason without stooping to the cultivation of the sentiments and affections. Never wonder. By means of addition, subtraction, multiplication and division, settle everything somehow, and never wonder. And yet, sitting with her brother in front of the fire at twilight, some weeks after Sissy's introduction into the household, Louisa fell prey to that great tempter, the imagination, and, staring into the embers, began to wonder.

Tom and Louisa are sitting by the fire in their study at Stone Lodge, Tom astride a chair

Tom I am sick of my life, Loo. I hate it altogether and I hate everybody except you.

Louisa You don't hate Sissy, Tom?

Tom She hates me.

Louisa No she does not, Tom, I am sure.

Tom She must. She must hate and detest the whole set-out of us. Already she's getting as pale as wax and as heavy as . . . I am. Look at me. I'm a donkey—obstinate, stupid and starved of pleasure. If only I could kick like one.

Louisa I hope you wouldn't kick me.

Tom Not you, Loo. I always make an exception of you. I don't know what this—prison—would be like without you.

Louisa Truly?

Tom Of course. What's the use of talking about it?

Louisa Because as I get older and nearer to growing up, I think more and more how little good I am to you. I can't play to you or sing to lighten your mind when you are tired. I can't even talk to you about anything amusing or interesting, because nothing ever happens to me.

Tom Well, I'm just as bad. Worse, because I'm stupid too. You're the only pleasure I have. You can brighten even this place.

Louisa You are a dear brother, Tom. Thank you. (*She kisses him*)

Tom I wish I could collect all the facts and figures we hear so much about, and all the people who found them out, and put a thousand barrels of gunpowder under them and blow them all up together. I'll have my revenge. When I go to live with Bounderby, I'll have my revenge.

Louisa Revenge?

Tom I mean I'll enjoy myself a little. I'll recompense myself for the way in which I have been brought up.

Louisa But Tom, Mr Bounderby thinks just as Father thinks. And he's not half so kind.

Tom Oh, I don't mind that. I know how to manage and smooth old Bounderby.

Louisa What is your great method of smoothing and managing, Tom? Is it a secret?

Tom Well, if it is a secret, it's not far off. It's you. You are his little pet, you are his favourite: he'll do anything for you. If he says anything I don't like, I shall say to him: "My sister Loo will be hurt and disappointed, Mr Bounderby. She told me you would be easier with me than this." That'll bring him round or nothing will.

A long pause. Louisa's face

Loo? Have you gone to sleep?

Louisa No, Tom, I am looking at the fire.

Tom You seem to find more to look at in it than ever I could find.

Louisa Tom, do you really look forward with any satisfaction to this change to Mr Bounderby's?

Tom Why, there's one thing to be said for it. It will be getting away from home.

Louisa Getting away from home. Yes.

Tom Of course, I shall be unwilling to leave you behind. But I must go whether I like it or not. And I had better go where I can take with me some advantage of your influence. Don't you see?

A long pause. Louisa stares into the fire

Louisa Yes Tom, I see.

Tom (*leaning on the back of her chair*) Except that it is a fire, it looks as stupid and blank as anything else does. What do you see in it? A circus?

Louisa I don't see anything in it particularly. But I have been wondering. About you and me, grown up.

Tom Wondering again.

Louisa I have such unmanageable thoughts that they will wonder. When I look at the red sparks dropping out of the fire and whitening and dying, it makes me think how short my life will be, and how little I can hope to do in it.

A moment. They look at one another

The Lights fade, then come up at once on Sissy

SCENE 7

Sissy I had a hard time of it, those first few months. Fact, fact, fact, all day long at school. Then, instead of going home to Father, to read to him stories about ogres and giants, it was back to Stone Lodge for more facts and figures and measurements. I decided to run away. But then I thought: if I run away, Father won't know where to find me when he comes back. So I had to stay. "Girl number twenty, name the cost of two hundred and forty-seven muslin caps at fourteen pence halfpenny." I was as low in the school as could be. But what could I do? They kept me at my learning and I became more miserable, but no wiser.

General light. Louisa is sitting reading in the study at Stone Lodge. Sissy approaches her

It would be a fine thing to be you, Miss Louisa.

Louisa Do you think so?

Sissy I should know so much. And all that is difficult to me now would be so easy.

Louisa You might not be the better for it.

Sissy I should not be the worse.

Louisa You are more useful to my mother, and more pleasant with her than I can ever be. You are pleasanter to yourself than I am to myself.

Sissy But I am—Oh so stupid. You don't know how stupid I am. All through school hours I make mistakes. I can't help them, they seem to come natural to me.

Louisa Tell me some of your mistakes.

Sissy I am ashamed. (*She pauses*) Today, the teacher was explaining about National Prosperity. And he said: "Now, this schoolroom is a Nation. And in this Nation there are fifty millions of money. Isn't that a prosperous nation? Girl number twenty, isn't that a prosperous nation, and an't you in a thriving state?"

Louisa What did you say?

Sissy I said I couldn't know whether it was a prosperous state or not, and whether I was in a thriving state or not, unless I knew who had got the money, and whether any of it was mine. But that had nothing to do with it, it was not in the figures at all.

Louisa That was a great mistake of yours.

Sissy Yes, Miss Louisa, I know it was. And the worst of all is, that although my father wished me so much to learn, I am afraid I don't like it.

Louisa Did he know so much himself that he wished you to be well taught too, Sissy?

Pause. They know this is a forbidden subject

No-one hears us.

Sissy Father . . . knows very little indeed. It's as much as he can do to write.

Louisa Your mother?

Sissy Father says she was quite a scholar. She died when I was born. She was . . . she was a dancer.

Louisa Did your father . . . love her?

Sissy Oh yes. Father loved me, first, for her sake. He carried me about with him when I was a baby. We have never been apart from that time.

Louisa Yet he leaves you now.

Sissy Only for my good. Nobody understands him as I do. He will not be happy for a single minute till he comes back.

Louisa And your father was always kind? To the last?

Sissy Always. Except one night. And that was not to me. He was angry with Merrylegs. The dog had failed to do one of his tricks that night. A jump on the backs of two chairs. Father ordered the dog to do the trick when he got in. The dog refused. Father beat him. There was blood everywhere. Father lay down on the floor and cried.

Sissy is sobbing. Louisa takes her hand and kisses her

Louisa I'm sorry, Sissy. Now that I've asked so much, please finish telling me how your father left you.

Sissy I came home from school that afternoon. Father sat rocking himself over the fire, in pain. I asked if he'd hurt himself, but he just said: "A little", and tried to hide his face from me. Then he said that he never gave the public satisfaction any more, he was a disgrace to the circus. I tried to cheer him by telling him all about school. When he'd listened his fill, he kissed me and asked me to fetch some of the oil he used for his hurts, and to get it at the best place, right over the other side of town. I asked him: "Shall I take Merrylegs?" but he said: "No, take nothing that's known to be mine." I left him sitting by the fire. Then the thought must have come upon him of going away to try something for my sake: when I came back, he was gone.

Louisa holds Sissy's hand for a moment

Sissy goes

Louisa (*out front*) After this, whenever Sissy dropped a curtsy to Mr Gradgrind in the presence of the family, and said in a faltering voice: "I beg your pardon, sir, for being troublesome, but have you had any letter yet about me?" Louisa would suspend the occupation of the moment and look for the reply as earnestly as Sissy did. And when Mr Gradgrind replied, as he always did: "No, Jupe, nothing of the sort", the trembling of Sissy's lip would be repeated in Louisa's face, and her eyes would follow Sissy with compassion to the door.

The Lights fade on Louisa then come up immediately on Actor 1

SCENE 8

Actor 1 In the hardest working part of Coketown; in the innermost
fortifications of that ugly citadel where nature was as strongly bricked out
as killing airs and gases were bricked in; at the heart of the labyrinth of
narrow courts upon courts, and close streets upon streets, which had
come into existence piecemeal, every piece in a violent hurry for some one
man's purpose, and the whole an unnatural family, shouldering and
trampling and pressing one another to death; in the last close nook of this
great exhausted receiver, where the chimneys, for want of air to make a
draught, were built in an immense variety of stunted and crooked shapes,
as though every house put out a sign of the kind of people who might be
expected to be born in it; here lives the multitude, the hands, a race who
would have found more favour with some people if Providence had seen
fit to make them only hands, or, like the lower creatures of the sea-shore,
only hands and stomachs.

Blackpool Amongst this multitude lived a certain Stephen Blackpool, forty
years of age.

*The whole company creates the effect of the Hands going home from work.
The audience should see a succession of quick cinematic images; two women
walking arm in arm; a young boy running; men bidding each other good-night
and going off in separate directions, etc. Perhaps a sound tape or live music to
emphasize the moment. The effect should be of a sudden change of focus as we
look for a moment at the mass of people in Coketown before returning to a
detailed examination of individuals. Eventually we pick out Stephen Blackpool, a serious-looking hand who seems older than he is. He is looking around
for Rachael. After a few moments he sees her ahead of him and runs to catch
up with her. She is a woman of thirty-five with gentle eyes and a quiet oval face*

Rachael!

Rachael Now then, lad.

Blackpool Thought as you were behind me. Early tonight?

Rachael Sometimes I'm early, sometimes I'm late. You can't count on me
going home.

Blackpool Nor in t' morning neither, I'm thinking.

Rachael Happen you're right.

They stop walking. She looks at him

You and me, eh, Stephen. Old friends. Ay, and getting to be old folk an'
all.

Blackpool Never you, Rachael. You look as young as ever.

Rachael Old friends. Too old to hide the truth. You and me, we shouldn't
walk together so much. Sometimes, ay, hard if we didn't sometimes——

Blackpool Hard enough as it is, Rachael.

Rachael Try not to think on it. That's best.

Blackpool I've tried not to think. Meks no difference. But you're right.
Folk'll talk. I'll do what you say. Allus do what you say, you've been that
good to me. Law to me, your word. Better than real laws, any road.

Rachael You leave the laws alone now, Stephen.

Blackpool Ay, I'll leave 'em alone. Leave all sorts alone. A muddle. A
muddle and there's an end of it.

Rachael Allus a muddle?
Blackpool (*laughing at himself*) Ay, allus. I come to the muddle over and over, but I never get beyond it.
Rachael Well, here's me. Good-night lad.
Blackpool Good-night, lass.

She goes

Good-night.
     When she was lost to view, he pursued his homeward way. He had had a hard life. It is said that every life has its roses and thorns; there seemed, however, to have been a misadventure or mistake in Stephen's case, whereby somebody else had become possessed of his roses, and he had become possessed of the same somebody else's thorns in addition to his own. He had known, to use his own words, a peck of trouble. He was usually called Old Stephen, in a kind of rough homage to the fact. A rather stooping man, with a knitted brow, a pondering expression of face, and a hard looking head, Old Stephen might have passed for a particularly intelligent man in his condition, yet he was not. Thousands of his compeers could talk much better than he, at any time. He was a good power-loom weaver, and a man of perfect integrity.

He goes into his home. The Lights are very low. There is a bed, perhaps suggested by benches

     As to his home, such as it was, it lay over a little shop. It was a neat room. The furniture was decent and sufficient, and though the atmosphere was tainted, the room was clean.

Suddenly a shape staggers towards Blackpool out of the gloom: Mrs Blackpool

     Heaven's mercy, woman, back again?
Mrs Blackpool Back again? Yes! And back again? And back again and again and again! Why not? Get away! Get away from the bed! That's mine by right. (*She slumps on to the bed*)
Blackpool He sunk into a chair, and moved but once all night. It was to throw a covering over her; as if his hands, shielding his eyes, were not enough to hide her, even in the darkness.

Black-out, then the Lights come up immediately

Scene 9

Blackpool The following day at noon, Stephen came out of the hot mill into the damp wind and cold, wet streets, haggard and worn. He turned from his own class and his own quarter towards the hill on which his principal employer lived, in a red house with black outside shutters and "Bounderby" upon a brazen plate at the front door. There was nothing troublesome against Stephen Blackpool, so he was admitted.

Bounderby's dining-room. Bounderby is sitting at a table having just finished lunch. Mrs Sparsit is at her needlework. Blackpool comes in

Bounderby Now, Stephen, what's the matter with you? We've never had any difficulty with you. You don't expect to be set up in a coach and six, and to be fed on turtle soup and venison, with a gold spoon, as a good many of 'em do! So I know already, you've not come here to make a complaint.

Blackpool Indeed I've not, sir.

Bounderby Well then, what have you got to say? Out with it.

Blackpool I've come to ask your advice. I've been wed nineteen year. To a lass that went to the bad. Not on account o' me, I've not been unkind to her.

Bounderby I've heard this before. She took to drinking, sold the furniture, pawned your clothes and so on.

Blackpool I was patient with her, but it went from bad to worse. She'd leave me, then come back. I paid her good money to stay away. These last five years. It's been hard for me, but I've had my peace of mind. Then, last night, I went home. There she is, lying on't hearthstone. Back again.

Bounderby I know all this. It's a bad job. You should not have got married. But there it is.

Mrs Sparsit Was it an unequal marriage, sir, in point of years?

Blackpool No, ma'am. I was twenty-one, she was twenty.

Mrs Sparsit Indeed. I inferred, from its being so miserable a marriage, that it was probably an unequal one in point of years.

Bounderby gives Mrs Sparsit a look

Blackpool I've come to ask you, sir, how am I to be rid of this woman?

Bounderby What do you mean? What are you saying? You took her for better or worse.

Blackpool I must be rid of her, sir. But for the pity and kind words I've had off the best lass living or dead, I'd have gone stark mad.

Mrs Sparsit (*low, to Bounderby*) I fear he wishes to be free to marry the female of whom he speaks.

Blackpool I do. That's right, what the lady says. I've read, in papers, about great folk getting themselves free of their misfortunate marriages. They get freed for smaller wrongs than mine. So I want to be rid of this woman, and I want to know how.

Bounderby Know how?

Blackpool If I do her any hurt, there's a law to punish me?

Bounderby Of course there is.

Blackpool If I flee from her, there's a law to punish me?

Bounderby Of course there is.

Blackpool If I marry t'other lass that's dear to me, there's a law to punish me?

Bounderby Of course there is.

Blackpool Now in God's name, show me the law that helps me.

Bounderby There is a sanctity in this relation of life, and it must be kept up.

Blackpool Mine's a grievous case, sir. I want to know the law that helps me.

Pause

Bounderby Now I tell you what. There is such a law.

Blackpool nods, hopeful

But it's not for you at all. It costs money. It costs a mint of money.

Blackpool How much might that be, sir?

Bounderby Why, by the time you've gone to Doctors' Commons with a suit, then to Common Law, then to the House of Lords, then got an Act of Parliament to enable you to re-marry, it would cost you—if it was a case of very plain-sailing—from a thousand to fifteen hundred pound. Perhaps twice as much.

Blackpool There's no other law?

Bounderby Certainly not.

Blackpool Why then, sir. It's a muddle. It's a muddle altogether, and the sooner I'm dead the better.

Mrs Sparsit tuts

Bounderby Don't talk nonsense, my good fellow, about things you don't understand. And don't you go calling the institutions of your country a muddle, or you'll get yourself into a real muddle one of those fine mornings. You didn't take your wife for fast or for loose, but for better or for worse. If she has turned out worse—why, all we have got to say is, she might have turned out better. I see traces of the turtle soup and venison with the gold spoon in this, by the Lord Harry I do.

Pause. Blackpool sighs

Blackpool Thank you, sir. I wish you good-day.

He goes

Bounderby Well, Mrs Sparsit?

Mrs Sparsit The vices of the people sir, the vices of the people. (*She shakes her head*)

The Lights fade on Mrs Sparsit and Bounderby and come up on Blackpool in the street outside

SCENE 10

Blackpool Old Stephen descended the two white steps, and crossed the street with his eyes bent upon the ground, and thus was walking sorrowfully away, when he felt a touch upon his arm.

Mrs Pegler steps forward. She is an old, kindly looking woman from the country in bright old-fashioned clothes

Mrs Pegler Pray, sir. Didn't I see you come out of that gentleman's house?

Blackpool That's right, missis.

Mrs Pegler Have you—you'll excuse an old woman's curiosity—seen the gentleman?

Blackpool Yes, missis.

Mrs Pegler And how did he look, sir? Was he portly, bold, outspoken and hearty?

Blackpool Oh yes, all of that.

Mrs Pegler And healthy?

Blackpool Eating and drinking as large as life.

Mrs Pegler Oh, thank you, thank you.

They walk together

Blackpool You'll find Coketown a busy place, I daresay.

Mrs Pegler Oh yes, dreadfully busy.

Blackpool You'll be from somewhere in the country yourself?

Mrs Pegler Yes. I came down by Parliamentary this morning, and I'm going back this afternoon. Forty miles here, forty miles back. I spend my savings so, once every year. I come regular, to tramp about the streets and see the gentlemen.

Blackpool Only to see 'em?

Mrs Pegler That's enough for me. I ask no more! I've been standing about on this side of the way, to see that gentleman you visited come out. But he's late this year, and I have not seen him. Still, I have seen you and you have seen him, and I must make that do. Are you going to work?

Blackpool Ay, at Bounderby's.

Mrs Pegler At Bounderby's?

Blackpool Ay, at Bounderby's, why?

Mrs Pegler An't you happy?

Blackpool Why, we all of us have our troubles, missis.

Mrs Pegler You have your troubles at home, you mean?

Blackpool Now and then.

Mrs Pegler But working under such a gentleman, they don't follow you to the factory?

Blackpool No, no. They don't follow me here.

They have reached the factory. They look up at it

Well ...

Mrs Pegler Will you shake hands with me before going in?

She offers her hand. He takes it

Blackpool Well. (*He turns to go*)

Mrs Pegler How long have you worked here?

Blackpool A dozen year.

Mrs Pegler I must kiss the hand that has worked in this fine factory for a dozen year.

Despite his embarrassment, she does so

Blackpool Now then.

He goes. They stand at opposite parts of the stage

(*Out front*) He had been at his loom full half an hour, thinking about this old woman, when, having occasion to move round the loom for its adjustment, he glanced through a window which was in his corner ...

Mrs Pegler (*out front*) And saw her still looking up at the pile of building, lost in admiration. Heedless of the smoke and mud and wet, and of her two long journeys, she was gazing at it, as if the heavy thrum that issued from its many storeys were proud music to her.

She goes off

Actor 1 comes on

SCENE 11

Actor 1 Time went on in Coketown like its own machinery: so much material wrought up, so much fuel consumed, so many powers worn out, so much money made. But, less inexorable than iron, steel or brass, it brought its varying seasons even into that wilderness of smoke and brick, and made the only stand that ever was made in the place against its direful uniformity. Time passed Tom on into Bounderby's bank, made him an inmate of Bounderby's house, necessitated the purchase of his first razor, and exercised him diligently in his calculations relative to number one. That same great manufacturer, Time, passed Sissy onwards in his mill, and worked her up into a very pretty article indeed.

Sissy and Gradgrind come on

Gradgrind I fear, Jupe, that your continuance any longer at the school would be useless.

Sissy I'm afraid it would, sir. I have tried hard, sir.

Gradgrind I believe you have. You are an affectionate, earnest, good young woman, and we must make that do.

Sissy I should wish for nothing if only my father——

Gradgrind That will do, Jupe! If your training in the science of reason had been more successful, we would long ago have heard the last on that subject.

Sissy and Gradgrind go

Actor 1 In some stages of his manufacture of the human fabric, the processes of time are very rapid. Tom and Sissy being both at such a stage in their working up, these changes were effected in a year or two: while Mr Gradgrind himself seemed stationary in his course and underwent no alteration, except that Time hustled him into a dirty by-corner, and made him Member of Parliament for Coketown. He also, at this time, made a discovery.

Louisa comes on from the other side of the stage. She walks slowly across Gradgrind's field of vision

Gradgrind Louisa is becoming a young woman.
Louisa is a young woman.
Louisa is a woman.

Louisa is now there, with Gradgrind

My dear. I must speak with you alone and seriously. Come to me in my room at breakfast tomorrow, will you?

Louisa Yes Father.

Gradgrind goes

So he kissed her and went away, and Louisa returned to the fireside to look at the short-lived sparks which so soon subsided into ashes.

Louisa sits. The Lights close in around her. Pause

(*To herself*) Dear Tom.

Tom's voice (*from off-stage, as if in her thoughts*) It would do me a great deal of good if you were to make up your mind to I know what, Loo. It would be a splendid thing for me. It would be uncommonly jolly.

The Lights come up. Gradgrind is standing in his study. Louisa sits, listening

Gradgrind Louisa my dear, you are the subject of a proposal of marriage that has been made to me.

Pause

A proposal of marriage, my dear.

Louisa I am attending, Father.

Gradgrind Perhaps you are not unprepared for the announcement I have it in charge to make.

Louisa I cannot say that, Father, until I hear it. Prepared or unprepared, I wish to hear it all from you. I wish to hear you state it to me.

Gradgrind Well then . . . I have undertaken to let you know that . . . that Mr Bounderby has informed me that he has long watched your progress with particular interest and pleasure, and has long hoped that the time might ultimately arrive when he should offer you his hand in marriage. That time is now come. Mr Bounderby has made his proposal of marriage to me, and has entreated me to make it known to you, and to express his hope that you will take it into your favourable consideration.

Silence

Louisa Father. Do you think I love Mr Bounderby?

Pause

Gradgrind My child . . . I really cannot take it upon myself to say.

Louisa Father, do you ask me to love Mr Bounderby?

Gradgrind My dear Louisa. (*He pauses*) No. I ask nothing.

Louisa Father. Does Mr Bounderby ask me to love him?

Gradgrind Really my dear, it is difficult to answer your question . . .

Louisa Yes or no, Father?

Gradgrind Difficult, because . . . because the reply depends so materially on the sense in which we use the expression. Mr Bounderby does not do you the injustice of pretending to anything fanciful, fantastic or sentimental. In these circumstances, the expression you used may be a little misplaced.

Louisa What would you advise me to use in its stead, Father?

Gradgrind I would advise you to consider the question, as you have been accustomed to consider every other question, simply as one of tangible Fact——

Louisa What would you recommend, Father, that I should substitute for the term I used just now? For the . . . misplaced expression?

Gradgrind Louisa. Nothing can be plainer. Confine yourself rigidly to Fact. The question of Fact to state to yourself is: "Does Mr Bounderby ask me to marry him?" Answer: "Yes, he does." The sole remaining question then is: "Shall I marry him?" I think nothing can be plainer than that.

Louisa "Shall I marry him?"

Gradgrind Precisely.

A pause. Louisa stares out of the window

Louisa The Coketown chimneys. There seems to be nothing there but smoke. But when night comes ... the fire ... bursts out ...

Gradgrind Louisa. Louisa. What is the application of that remark?

Louisa What does it matter? What does it matter? Since Mr Bounderby likes to take me thus, I am satisfied to accept his proposal. Tell him, as soon as you please, that this was my answer. Repeat it word for word. I should wish him to know what I said.

Gradgrind I will observe your request, my dear. It is quite right to be exact. Have you any wish as to the date of your wedding?

Louisa None. What does it matter?

Pause

Gradgrind Louisa. I have not considered it essential to ask one question because the possibility implied in it appeared to me to be much too remote. But perhaps I ought to do so. You have never entertained in secret any other proposal?

Louisa What other proposal can have been made to me? Whom have I seen? Where have I been? What are my heart's experiences?

Pause

Gradgrind You correct me justly. I merely wished to discharge my duty.

Louisa What do I know of tastes and fancies; of aspirations and affections; of all that part of my nature in which such light things might have been nourished? What escape have I had from problems that could be demonstrated and realities that could be grasped? (*She tightens her hand, then slowly unclenches it*) What a question to ask *me*? You have been so careful of me that I never had a child's heart. You have trained me so well that I never dreamed a child's dream. You have dealt so wisely with me that I never had a child's belief or a child's fear.

Gradgrind My dear Louisa. You abundantly repay my care. Kiss me, my dear girl.

She kisses him

Now. Let us go and find your mother.

They go. Then Louisa breaks away

Gradgrind exits

Louisa (*out front*) Mrs Gradgrind was accordingly found and informed, the news occasioning feeble signs of animation in her recumbent form. But Sissy, who was working beside her and heard of the engagement in the same instant, suddenly turned her head and looked, in wonder, in pity, in sorrow, in doubt, in a multitude of emotions towards Louisa. Louisa had known it, and seen it, without looking at her. From that moment, she was impassive, proud and cold—held Sissy at a distance—changed to her altogether.

Louisa goes

Actor 1 comes on immediately

Actor 1 Mr Bounderby's first disquietude, on hearing of his happiness, was occasioned by the necessity of imparting it to Mrs Sparsit. He could not make up his mind how to do that, or what the consequences of the step might be. Whether she would instantly depart bag and baggage to Lady Scadgers, or would positively refuse to budge from the premises; whether she would be plaintive or abusive, tearful or tearing; whether she would break her heart or break the looking-glass; Mr Bounderby could not at all foresee. On his way home, on the evening he set aside for telling her this momentous news, he took the precaution of stepping into a chemist's shop and buying a bottle of the very strongest smelling salts. "By George", thought Mr Bounderby, "if she takes it in the fainting way, I'll have the skin off her nose at all events." But in spite of being thus forearmed, he entered his own house with anything but a courageous air; and appeared before the object of his misgivings like a dog who was conscious of coming direct from the pantry.

He becomes Bounderby. Mrs Sparsit is sitting by the fire, picking holes in a piece of cambric with the points of her scissors

Mrs Sparsit Good-evening Mr Bounderby.
Bounderby Good-evening, ma'am, good-evening.

Bounderby draws his chair close to the fire. Mrs Sparsit draws hers further away

Don't go to the North Pole, ma'am.
Mrs Sparsit Thank you, sir. (*She moves her chair back, though short of its former position*)
Bounderby Mrs Sparsit, ma'am. I have no occasion to say to you, that you are not only a lady born and bred, but a devilish sensible woman.
Mrs Sparsit Sir, this is not the first time that you have honoured me with similar expressions of your good opinion.
Bounderby Mrs Sparsit ma'am. I am going to astonish you. (*He is on his feet, reaching for the stopper of the smelling salts, concealed behind his back*)
Mrs Sparsit (*calmly*) Yes sir? (*She lays down her work and smooths her mittens*)
Bounderby I am going, ma'am, to marry Tom Gradgrind's daughter.
Mrs Sparsit (*immediately*) Yes sir? I hope you may be happy, Mr Bounderby. I hope indeed you may be happy.

Bounderby, who has the stopper off the smelling salts and is ready to administer them, is astonished by her tranquillity, and furtively conceals the bottle

Bounderby Ah!
Mrs Sparsit Yes sir, I wish with all my heart that you may, in all respects be very happy.
Bounderby Well, ma'am. I am obliged to you. I hope I shall be.
Mrs Sparsit *Do* you sir? But naturally you do. Of course you do.

Pause. Mrs Sparsit resumes her work. She coughs in a small, triumphant way

Bounderby Well, ma'am, under these circumstances, I imagine it would not be agreeable to a character like yours to remain here. Though you would, of course, be very welcome. If you did.

Mrs Sparsit Oh dear, no sir. I could on no account think of that. (*She coughs again*)

Bounderby However, ma'am, there are apartments at the bank where a born and bred lady as keeper of the place would be rather a catch than otherwise; and if the same terms——

Mrs Sparsit I beg your pardon, sir. You were so good as to promise that you would always substitute the phrase "annual compliment".

Bounderby I apologize, ma'am. Annual compliment. If the same annual compliment would be acceptable there, I see nothing to part us—unless you do.

Mrs Sparsit Sir, if the position I should assume at the bank is one that I could occupy without descending lower in the social scale——

Bounderby Why of course it is. If it was not, you would not suppose I would offer it to a lady who has moved in the society you have moved in.

Mrs Sparsit You are very considerate, sir.

Bounderby You'll have your own private apartments, a maid and a light porter, and you'll be what I take the liberty of considering precious comfortable.

Mrs Sparsit Sir, say no more. I accept your offer gratefully and with many sincere acknowledgements of past favours. And I hope sir, I fondly hope, that Miss Gradgrind may be all you desire and deserve. (*She beams at him*)

The Lights fade, then come up immediately

SCENE 13

The wedding. All available actors become wedding guests

Actress 1 And so the day came: and when it came, there were married . . .

Actor 1 Josiah Bounderby of Coketown . . .

Actress 2 To Louisa . . .

Actor 2 Daughter of Thomas Gradgrind Esquire of Stone Lodge, MP for that borough.

Bounderby and Louisa in a wedding tableau. Cries of "Speech, speech." Bounderby takes centre stage perhaps standing on a raised platform or chair. Louisa stands watching him. The other actors melt into the audience, who become wedding guests. Bounderby holds up a hand

Bounderby Ladies and gentlemen. I am Josiah Bounderby of Coketown. If you want a speech this morning, my friend and father-in-law, Tom Gradgrind, is a member of parliament, so you know where to get it.

Laughter

I am not your man. Still, since you have done my wife and myself the honour of drinking our health and happiness, I suppose I must acknowledge the same. (*He clears his throat*) If I feel a little independent when I look around this gathering today, and reflect how little I thought of marrying Tom Gradgrind's daughter when I was a ragged street-boy who never washed his face unless it was at a pump, and that not oftener than once a fortnight, I hope I may be excused. So I hope you like my feeling independent; if you don't, I can't help it. I *do* feel independent.

Laughter

Now I have mentioned and you have mentioned that I am this day married to Tom Gradgrind's daughter. I am very glad to be so. I believe she is worthy of me. And I believe I am worthy of her. So I thank you, on both our parts, for the goodwill you have shown towards us: and the best wish I can give the unmarried part of the present company is this: I hope every bachelor may find as good a wife as I have found. And I hope every spinster may find as good a husband as my wife has found. Thank you.

Actor 2 A toast to the bride and groom!

All The bride and groom!

Louisa joins her husband. Tableau

Actress 1 Shortly after which oration, as they were going on a nuptial trip to Lyons, the happy pair departed for the railroad.

Bounderby goes off

The bride in passing down the stairs found Tom waiting for her.

Tom comes forward, flushed with drink. He has a brandy glass and a cigar

Tom What a game girl you are, Loo, to be such a first-rate sister!

She holds him tightly, her feelings only just in check

Come on now. Time's up. Old Bounderby's quite ready. Goodbye, I shall be on the look-out for you, when you come back. My dear Loo, an't it uncommonly jolly now! (*He moves away*) An't it uncommonly jolly!

He goes

Louisa stands, alone. She stares ahead. The Lights fade

END OF BOOK THE FIRST

SCENE 14

Actress 2 Book the Second: "Reaping".

Actor 2 A sunny midsummer day. There was such a thing sometimes, even in Coketown.

Mrs Sparsit's apartment at the bank. She sits at the window, a table at her side

Mrs Sparsit At the bank, Mrs Sparsit sat in her afternoon apartment, from which post of observation, she was ready every morning, to greet Mr Bounderby as he came across the road, with the sympathizing recognition appropriate to a victim. He had been married now a year; and Mrs Sparsit had never released him from her determined pity a moment.

Actor 1 Mrs Sparsit's tea was set for her on a pert little table. The light porter placed the tea-tray on it, knuckling his forehead as a form of homage. He was a very light porter indeed; as light as in the days when he defined a horse for girl number twenty.

Mrs Sparsit Thank you, Bitzer.

Bitzer Thank you, ma'am.

Mrs Sparsit All is shut up, Bitzer?

Bitzer All is shut up, ma'am.

Mrs Sparsit And what is the news of the day? Anything in particular?

Bitzer Well, ma'am. I can't say that I have heard anything in particular.

Mrs Sparsit The clerks.

Bitzer Yes, ma'am?

Mrs Sparsit Are they trustworthy? Punctual? Industrious?

Bitzer Yes, ma'am, pretty fair. With the usual exception.

Mrs Sparsit Aaah.

Bitzer Master Thomas, ma'am. I doubt Master Thomas very much, ma'am. I don't like his ways at all.

Mrs Sparsit Bitzer. I have spoken to you in the past respecting . . . names.

Bitzer I beg your pardon, ma'am. It's quite true, you did object to names being used. And you're right. They are best avoided.

Mrs Sparsit I hold a trust here, Bitzer. And I cannot have the trust Mr Bounderby places in me shaken by mention under this roof, of names that are—unfortunately—connected with his.

Bitzer I beg your pardon, ma'am, I do beg your pardon.

Mrs Sparsit Say "an individual" and I will hear you. Say "Master Thomas" and you must excuse me.

Bitzer Yes, ma'am. (*He pauses*) The clerks are trustworthy . . . punctual . . . and industrious. (*He pauses*) With the exception of an individual.

Mrs Sparsit Aaah!

Bitzer I only hope, ma'am, that his friend and relation may not supply him with the means of carrying on. Otherwise ma'am, we know out of whose pocket *that* money comes.

Mrs Sparsit Aa-aah!

Bitzer He is to be pitied, ma'am.

Mrs Sparsit is puzzled

The last party I alluded to is to be pitied, ma'am.

Mrs Sparsit understands

Mrs Sparsit Yes, Bitzer. I have always pitied him. Always.

Bitzer (*dropping his voice*) As to an individual, ma'am. He is as improvident as any of the people in this town. And you know what *their* improvidence is, ma'am. No-one could wish to know it better than a lady of your eminence does.

Mrs Sparsit They would do well to take example by you, Bitzer.

Bitzer Thank you, ma'am. (*He knuckles his forehead*) Would you wish a little hot water, ma'am, or is there anything else I could fetch you?

Mrs Sparsit Nothing just now, Bitzer.

Bitzer Thank you, ma'am. I shouldn't wish to disturb you at your meals, ma'am, particularly tea, knowing your partiality for it, but there's a gentleman been looking up here for a minute or so, ma'am, and he has come across as if he was going to knock. That *is* his knock, ma'am, no doubt.

Mrs Sparsit A gentleman? Show him in, Bitzer, show him in!

Actor 1 The gentleman being shown in, introduced himself as Mr James Harthouse, an acquaintance of Mr Gradgrind, and desirous of locating the residence of Mr Bounderby, and wondering if the superior-looking lady gracing the upper windows of the same Bounderby's bank would be able to assist.

Mrs Sparsit Not only did Mrs Sparsit direct the stranger to his goal, she also disabused him of the mistaken notion that Mrs Bounderby was a grim matron of five and fifty.

Actor 1 On learning that Louisa had not yet reached one and twenty, a sudden light of interest flickered in Mr James Harthouse's languid eye ...

Mrs Sparsit A circumstance which so impressed Mrs Sparsit, that later, as she negotiated a passage through her nocturnal sweetbread, she paused for a moment and exclaimed: "Oh you fool!" Whom she meant, she did not say. But she could scarcely have meant the sweetbread.

The Lights fade out on Mrs Sparsit

SCENE 15

The Lights came up on Harthouse. He is a man of the world, "five-and-thirty, good-looking, good figure, good teeth, good voice, good breeding". He is standing in Bounderby's library skimming through a book

    Louisa comes in

Louisa Mr James Harthouse?

He turns

    I am Mrs Bounderby. My husband and I are very pleased to have you as our guest tonight.

Harthouse Mrs Bounderby, it is I who am pleased, not to say honoured.

Louisa I hope you do not take exception to being entertained by a woman. You will have observed that my husband was called away upon a matter of business as soon as you arrived. And my brother Tom has not yet returned from the bank.

Harthouse On the contrary, entertainment by the fair sex constitutes, in my eyes, the greatest entertainment of all, and in this particular instance, your reputation as a woman of——

Louisa Quite so, Mr Harthouse. And what brings you to Coketown?

Harthouse What indeed? I was putting the same question to myself this afternoon when proceeding through the gloom of your streets after alighting from the train.

Louisa And what answer did you make yourself, Mr Harthouse?

Harthouse I . . . well, let me put it this way. I have a brother——

Louisa In the House of Commons, yes. John Harthouse. It was my father, I believe who was instrumental in introducing you via your brother to my husband.

Harthouse Ye-es. Well Jack . . . or John as you so properly nominate him . . . thought there might be an opening for me among the . . . hard fact men. He put it to me that I might go in for statistics. So. I coached myself up with a blue book or two, made a few dashes in the public meeting way and . . . here I am.

Louisa Indeed. But you have . . . gone in for things before now, have you not?

Harthouse Oh rather. I was a Cornet of Dragoons till I became bored with it and took up the foreign office and found that . . .

Louisa A bore?

Harthouse Oh indeed. A bore of very substantial proportions. So I travelled to Jerusalem and got bored there, since when I've been yachting round the world.

Louisa And how was that?

Harthouse Oh, *ennuyant, très ennuyant.*

Louisa And you have come up here to show the nation the way out of its difficulties.

Harthouse Mrs Bounderby, upon my honour, no. I will make no such pretence to you. I have seen a little, here and there, up and down. I have found it all to be worthless, as everybody has, and as some confess they have and some do not, and I am going in for your father's respected opinions—really because I have no choice of opinions and may as well fall back on your father's as anybody else's.

Louisa Have you none of your own?

Harthouse I have not so much as the slightest predilection left. I assure you, I attach not the least importance to opinions. The result of the varieties of boredom I have undergone, is a conviction that any set of ideas will do just as much good as any other set: "What will be, will be"—it's the only truth going.

Pause. Louisa is marginally impressed

Louisa I see.

Pause

Harthouse Quite a fine library you have here.

Louisa It is a large library, Mr Harthouse. (*She goes towards him and looks at the book he has selected*) Euclid. You see, Mr Harthouse, my mind was formed on quite different truths from "What will be, will be".

A stylized freeze. Louisa holds the book, Harthouse walks around her, admiring

Harthouse Is there nothing? Is there nothing that will move that lovely face?

Tom comes in

Louisa unfreezes. She's overjoyed to see him

Louisa Tom!

She runs to him, holds his hands and kisses him. Freeze

Harthouse Ay, ay! This whelp she cares for. How great must be the solitude of her heart to bestow it on a sullen young oaf such as this.

Louisa and Tom come forward

Louisa Mr James Harthouse. My brother Tom.

Harthouse and Tom shake hands

Louisa looks at them for a moment and then exits

Harthouse James Harthouse encouraged Tom throughout the course of the evening and showed an unusual liking for him.

Tom Tom, in response, was at his very wittiest, taking no pains to hide his contempt for Mr Bounderby by making wry faces and winking behind his brother-in-law's back.

Harthouse When Harthouse finally rose to go, the whelp immediately proffered his services as guide. Arriving at the hotel, Harthouse asked him to come up.

Tom And Tom could do no less than comply with this request.

SCENE 16

Instantly Harthouse and Tom are in the hotel room. A couple of chairs

Harthouse Do you smoke?
Tom Well, Mr Harthouse, I don't know but that I won't.

Tom takes a proffered cigar

Harthouse And you're drinking next to nothing, Tom, come on!

Harthouse fills Tom's glass with brandy

Tom Thank'ee. Thank'ee, Mr Harthouse. Well, I hope you have had about a dose of Old Bounderby tonight. (*He shuts one eye, and looks knowingly over his glass at Harthouse*)
Harthouse A very good fellow indeed.
Tom (*winking again*) You think so, don't you?
Harthouse What a comical brother-in-law you are!
Tom What a comical brother-in-law old Bounderby is, I think you mean.
Harthouse You are a piece of caustic, Tom.
Tom Oh! I don't care for old Bounderby if you mean that. I have always

called him Old Bounderby and I am not going to begin to be polite now.

Harthouse Don't mind me, old man, but take care when his wife is by, you know.

Tom His wife! My sister, Loo? Oh yes! (*He helps himself to more brandy*) *She* never cared for Old Bounderby either.

Harthouse That's the past tense, Tom. We are in the present tense now.

Tom Verb neuter, not to care. Indicative mood, present tense. First person singular, I do not care; second person singular thou dost not care; third person singular, she does not care.

Harthouse (*applauding*) Very good! Very quaint! But you don't mean it.

Tom But I *do* mean it. Upon my honour! Why, you won't tell me, Mr Harthouse, that you really suppose my sister Loo does care for Old Bounderby.

Harthouse My dear fellow, what am I bound to suppose, when I find two married people living together in harmony and happiness?

Tom (*putting his feet up*) Loo never had a lover, and when the governor proposed Old Bounderby, she took him.

Harthouse That was very dutiful in your interesting sister.

Tom Yes, but she wouldn't have been as dutiful, and it would not have come off so easily, if it hadn't been for me.

Harthouse raises his eyebrows and waits

I persuaded her. I was stuck into Old Bounderby's bank, and I knew I should get into scrapes here if she put Old Bounderby's pipe out; so I told her my wishes and she came into them. She would do anything for me. It was very game of her, wasn't it?

Harthouse It was charming, Tom.

Tom Not that it was altogether so important to her as it was to me, because my liberty and comfort and getting on depended on it; and she had no other lover, and staying at home was like staying in jail—especially when I was gone. It wasn't as if she gave up another lover for Old Bounderby; but still, it was a good thing in her.

Harthouse Perfectly delightful. And she gets on so placidly.

Tom Oh, she's a regular girl. A girl can get on anywhere. She has settled down to the life and *she* don't mind. It does just as well as any other. Besides, though Loo is a girl, she's not a common sort of girl. She can shut herself up within herself and think, watching the fire for hours at a stretch.

Harthouse Ay, ay. Has resources of her own, eh?

Tom Not so much as you may suppose, for our governor has had her crammed with all sorts of dry bones and sawdust. It's his system.

Harthouse Formed his daughter on his own model?

Tom His daughter? He forms everybody on his own model. Why, he formed me that way.

Harthouse Impossible.

Tom 'S true. When I first left home, I was as flat as a warming pan. Knew no more about life than an oyster.

Harthouse Come, Tom, I can hardly believe that. A joke's a joke.

Tom I'm serious. I am indeed. Oh I've picked up a little since, I don't deny it. But I've done it myself, no thanks to the governor.

Harthouse And your intelligent sister?

Tom Oh, *she* don't mind. Girls can always get on somehow.

Harthouse Calling at the bank yesterday evening, I found an ancient lady there who seems to entertain great admiration for your sister.

Tom Mother Sparsit! What! You have seen her already, have you? (*He shuts his eye again and taps his nose with his finger*) Mother Sparsit's feeling for Loo is more than admiration I should think. Say affection and devotion. Mother Sparsit never set her cap at Bounderby when he was a bachelor. Oh no!

Tom gradually subsides during this last into a snooze. Harthouse stands looking at him, then goes over and stirs Tom with his boot

Harthouse Come, it's late. Be off.

Tom wakes with a start

Tom Mmmm. Yes. I must take my leave of you. (*He sits, shaking his head*) Mmmm. I must say. Your tobacco. Very good tobacco. Very good. But it's too mild.

Harthouse You're quite right, Tom. It is. Too mild.

Tom Ridiculously mild.

Harthouse Quite so, Tom.

Tom Now then, where's the door? Ah! Good-night!

Harthouse Good-night, Tom.

Tom goes

Harthouse stands a moment, then goes

Actor 2 returns

Actor 2 The whelp went home and went to bed. If he had had any sense of what he had done that night, and had been less of a whelp and more of a brother, he might have turned short on the road, might have gone down to the ill-smelling river that was dyed black, might have gone to bed in it for good and all, and have curtained his head for ever in its filthy waters.

As the Lights fade, we hear the noise of the crowd waiting for the start of the Union meeting

Scene 17

The Union Meeting. A crowded hall. It may be most effective for any available actors to take up positions among the audience so that the audience feel like participants in the meeting. The speeches of Slackbridge and Mary Stokes are punctuated by applause from the floor. This should be done by stamping on the floor and hammering on any resonant surfaces available rather than by hand-clapping

Chairwoman Order, order! Friends, brothers and sisters. I declare this meeting of the Union of Coketown Weavers open. Now you'll all be knowing the main piece of business before us this evening. We've got one weaver, just one on us out of all in Coketown, who won't join Union. Now this piece o' business has been in all our minds some time now, and we've got Mr Slackbridge, delegate from Union up to say his piece on't subject first. Mr Slackbridge.

Applause. Slackbridge takes the floor

Slackbridge My friends and fellow workers of Coketown. It is understandable when opposition to our Union comes from the side of the masters. After all, it's their excess profits that we seek to turn into higher wages for our own kind. It is a good deal less understandable when a working-man, a hand, a weaver of Coketown, who is practically acquainted with the wrongs and grievances of you all, should fail to subscribe to the funds of the Union of Coketown Weavers and stand alone in such a way as to endanger the triumph of our whole great enterprise. Our Union is founded on the strength and resolve of its members: one weak link in the chain and the whole chain is spoiled. Now I hear you say: "What are we to do?" If this man will not join us, if he persists in his stubborn path of standing aloof from our gallant stand for Freedom and for Right, should we not let him alone and hope that he comes to his senses in the longer run? Should we not wait until he is shamed into joining when he sees the positive benefits that will accrue from his membership of the Union? Why should we expend so much time and trouble on this one sheep who is too stubborn, or too stupid, or too much a friend of the masters to join our fold? Well I'll tell you why, if any of you has your doubts. I'll tell you why you should trouble yourselves to take action against this man: because there is a principle at stake, a vital principle. What we have, today, in Coketown, in the North, in the whole of Britain, is a struggle. Not a negotiation, or a compromise or a co-operative agreement: a struggle. And as a matter of principle, we, in this Union, want no dealings with folk who won't say what side they're on. A weaver who won't stand by his own when the masters are putting forward a proposal for a ten per cent cut in wages, is like an infantryman who, when the enemy is massed and the command given, says to his colleagues: "Look here, I don't think I'll be joining you in this charge." If you here in Coketown are going to make a serious fight to improve your wages, your standard of living and your conditions of employment, then you cannot merely stand aside when one of your own refuses to help you in your struggle.

Slackbridge sits. Thunderous applause

Chairwoman Thank you, Mr Slackbridge. Well, we'll not have men accused and not allowed to stand up and speak for themselves, not while I'm running meetings. So I'm calling next on the man in question to come forward. You all know him. Stephen Blackpool.

Blackpool comes forward. He is diffident at first, but becomes increasingly confident. His speech is heard in silence

Blackpool Like's been said, you all know me, Stephen Blackpool. Weaver at Bounderby's now for a dozen year, near as meks no difference. And it's true, I'm only one as won't come in with proposed regulations. Well, you've heard Mr Slackbridge. He's the delegate, it's his trade to speak, and he does it well. Only I must take up against summat he said, though I'll not put it as well as he does, being just a weaver, and never pretended to be more. I go along with Mr Slackbridge until he uses one word: struggle. He says how it's the natural way of things for weavers to struggle against masters, that there must always, between the two sides, be a conflict, a war. Well I say this to Mr Slackbridge: weavers need masters as much as masters need weavers. It's masters as creates the jobs for us to do. It's masters as builds factories. It's masters as finds a sale for what we mek wi' our hands. Ay, I believe in a Union—Union between masters and workers, that's what I believe in. Our wages come out of masters' profits. And if we produce too much and demand falls and masters' profits fall, then our share must fall too. That's a law, just like throwin' stone in air and it comin' down is a law, and you'll not alter that with your talk of struggle. Ay, times is hard, course they are. But it's not your struggle, your conflict and your strike as'll mek 'em better: they'll more likely do you harm. Only thing as'll make times better is harmony, peace, co-operation, Christian brotherhood. And that's why I'll not join Union. 'Cos all your Slackbridges and your other delegates'll do nowt but lead whole set of us down road to ruin. And that's all I've got to say.

Complete silence. He stands down

Chairwoman Well, Mr Slackbridge has had his say, and Stephen Blackpool's had his. Anyone else from the floor wish to speak.

Mary Stokes comes forward. Frequent stamping, hammering and cheering greet her speech as soon as its drift becomes clear

Mary My name's Mary Stokes and I'm a four-loom weaver at Bounderby's as most on you know. Now Stephen Blackpool's said as 'ow we all ought to come together, workers and masters, all in a spirit of co-operation. Well that's a notion as I'd like to support. Ay and I will support it when I see masters coming in six days a week at half-past six in t' morning and going off home at half-past seven at night. I'll stand up for Christian brotherhood when I see masters going home with ten shilling a week in their pockets. I'll be on t' side of peace and harmony when I hear of masters sleeping six to a room wi' nowt in their bellies and no place else to mek a living. Stephen Blackpool says as how we owe masters a livin', because they give us factories to work in and sell us work. Well I tell him this. We *have* to work in factories 'cos our own living was took off us by masters. My grandmother nivver had to work in no factory. She and her family worked at home, and when they finished a piece, they went to market and sold it themselves. Bounderby and his like haven't given us our living, they've took it away. Ay, and time'll come when we tek it back off 'em. What I have to say to Stephen Blackpool is that he can't see what's set plain in front of his own face. And if he'll not stand by the likes of us, then I say this, we'll not stand by the likes of him. He's been given his chance, not just tonight, but many's the time this last year. And with masters coming forward now with proposals for a cut in wages, I say we must all stand together. Now I don't say as we should tek the man's livelihood away: but I do say as if Stephen Blackpool wants to stand by 'imself, that's the way the rest of us want it too: and I move that we should send him to Coventry and have nowt more to do wi' him.

Applause. She stands down

Chairwoman Meeting'll now move to a vote on Mary Stokes's motion. Those in favour . . .

Much hammering and stamping

Those against . . .

Total silence

The motion is clearly carried. Stephen Blackpool is now in Coventry.

The meeting dissolves. Blackpool is alone in a spotlight

Blackpool Four days. Not a word. To a soul. From a soul. Not even daring to go near Rachael. Out of fear of her being cast out too. End of fourth day. Leaving mill. Young lad comes up. Name of Bitzer. Light porter at bank. Message. Mr Bounderby wanting to see Stephen Blackpool. Now.

His spot goes out. The Lights come up immediately on Scene 18

SCENE 18

Bounderby's dining-room. The setting should be the same as for Scene 9

Bounderby is pacing, waiting for Blackpool. Louisa sits impassively

Blackpool comes in

Bounderby Well, Blackpool. What's this I hear? What have these pests of the earth been doing to you? Speak up.

Blackpool is confused

Blackpool What were you wanting with me, sir?

Bounderby Why, I have told you. Speak up and tell us about yourself and this combination.

Blackpool Beg your pardon, sir, but I've nowt to say about it.

Bounderby Nothing to say? I suppose you've nothing to say about this Slackbridge being in town, stirring up a mutiny.

Blackpool I'm as sorry as you are, sir, when the people's leaders are bad. Happen it's not the worst of their misfortunes.

Bounderby May I take the liberty of asking how it happens that you refuse to be in this combination?

Blackpool It's not my belief, sir, and that's all about it. It's not in my nature to combine. I stand alone, sir.

Bounderby So you agree that these people are a set of rascals and rebels whom transportation is too good for?

Blackpool Nay, sir. Not rascals or rebels or owt like that. They've done me no kindness, God knows, but I'll not fail to stand by 'em now, whatever they've done to me. They're good people.

Bounderby So full of virtue they've cut you adrift. Go through with it, man, while you're about it.

Blackpool They're good, patient people, and they want, in the main to do right. If there's trouble, well, I can't think the fault is allus with us.

Bounderby is enraged

Bounderby I see. The fault is not always with the people, eh? Listen to this, Louisa. So what are you complaining about?

Blackpool I didn't come here to complain. I came 'cos I was sent for.

Bounderby But what in general do your people complain of? (*After a pause*) Eh?

Pause. Blackpool hesitates, then takes the plunge

Blackpool Take a look at this town. Coketown. Take a look at the people who were born here, live here, die here. Weaving, carding, piecing out a living. And look at all those as comes to talk about us, write about us, send deputations to secretary of state about us. And how they allus come to the same conclusion. You're always in the right, we're always in the wrong.

Bounderby I hear mischievous strangers in this, by the Lord Harry I do.

Blackpool Mischievous strangers! When have we not heard of these mischievous strangers. It's not them that *makes* the trouble. It doesn't begin with *them*. Don't get me wrong, I've got no love for them, neither. But you could drop all the Slackbridges in the world into the deepest ocean and the muddle'd still be there. Look, I'm not a clever man, so I can't tell you what will better all this. But I'll tell you what won't and that's conflict. What'll do it is compromise, working together in harmony, workers and masters, that's what'll do it. Ay, and that can only happen when you stop treating the hands like figures in a sum. Till God's work is unmade, sir, it'll not do to pretend that your hands are nothing but hands; they've hearts and minds too, sir, not just hands: hearts, minds and souls.

Bounderby This is the old gold spoon and venison business, this is the gold spoon look-out in a different garb.

Blackpool I tell you, sir, it's not.

Bounderby It's clear to me that you are one of those fellows that's always got a grievance. You go about sowing discord and raising mutiny. That's the business of your life, my friend. You're such a waspish, raspish, ill-conditioned chap, that even your own people will have nothing to do with you. I never thought these fellows could be right in anything, but I tell you what! I so far go along with them for a novelty, that *I'll* have nothing to do with you neither.

Blackpool looks up at him quickly

You can finish the piece you're on, and then you can go.

Blackpool Sir. If I can't get work from you, I'll not be able to get it elsewhere.

Bounderby That's not my concern. What I know, I know; and what you know, you know. That's my last word on the subject.

Blackpool looks at Louisa. She looks away

Blackpool Heaven help us all in this world.

He turns and goes

Louisa looks at Bounderby

Bounderby The gold spoon.

Quick Black-out

SCENE 19

The Lights come up on Blackpool

Blackpool On leaving Mr Bounderby's, Stephen Blackpool's first impulse was to seek out Rachael. He found her on the way home, accompanied by Mrs Pegler, the strange old woman, who had been paying her annual visit to Coketown in hope of catching a glimpse of Mr Bounderby. Rachael took the news of Stephen Blackpool's dismissal quietly, both of them forgetting their troubles in their concern for Mrs Pegler's well-being. All three had repaired to Stephen's room for tea when the landlady announced a visit by Louisa Bounderby. Mrs Pegler, disconcerted to a degree by this surprising occurrence, withdrew into the shadows, as Louisa, accompanied at a distance by her brother, came into the room.

Blackpool's room. Blackpool and Rachael are there. (If there are more than two actresses in the company, Mrs Pegler should be present also)

Louisa comes in. She addresses Stephen

Louisa I have come to speak to you in consequence of what passed just now. I should like to be serviceable to you, if you will let me. Is this your wife?

Rachael raises her eyes, then lowers them again

(*Embarrassed*) I remember. I recollect now, to have heard your domestic misfortunes spoken of. It was not my meaning to ask a question that would give pain to anyone here.

Pause. Louisa decides to speak to Blackpool through Rachael

He ... has told you what has passed between himself and my husband? You would be his first recourse, I think?

Rachael I have heard the end of it.

Louisa Did I understand that being rejected by one employer, he would probably be rejected by all?

Rachael A man who gets a bad name among 'em hasn't a lot of chance.

Louisa A bad name?

Rachael Ay, that of troublemaker.

Louisa Then by the prejudices of his own class and by the prejudices of the other, he is sacrificed alike? Are the two so deeply separated in this town, that there is no place whatever for an honest workman between them?

Rachael shakes her head. Louisa turns to Blackpool

What will you do?

Blackpool Quit this part, try another. A man can but try. If yo' leave off tryin', there's nowt to do but lay down and die.

Louisa And ... how will you travel?

Blackpool On foot.

Louisa gets her purse out. She takes out a banknote and offers it to Rachael

Louisa Rachael, is it?
Rachael Yes, ma'am.
Louisa Will you tell him that this is freely his to help him on his way? Will you entreat him to take it?
Rachael It's not for me to do, young lady. Bless yo' for thinkin' of 'im. But only he knows his own heart and what seems right or wrong to it.

Louisa turns to Blackpool. She is embarrassed, nervous. He is moved

Blackpool I can't tek that. Not that much. I'll tek two pound. Ay, borrow it. Borrow it and pay back. And God bless you, young lady. I couldn't be more thankful.

Louisa retracts the note, hands him two pounds in coins

Louisa I hope, wherever you may go, that you may find greater fortune than you have left behind you in Coketown.
Actor 1 At this point, Tom, who had been watching the interview progress with no sign of interest, suddenly motioned to Blackpool to follow him out on to the stairs. Discovering that Blackpool would remain in Coketown for another three days, the whelp suggested to him that it would be immensely to Blackpool's advantage, if, on the following three evenings, he would loiter in the vicinity of the bank immediately after work, awaiting a message from Bitzer which might yield him unexpected returns. Tom earnestly counselled Blackpool not to speak to anyone unless spoken to, and to go on his way after an hour should nothing accrue from his waiting. And with this mysterious offer of help conveyed, the whelp was in the street and calling for his sister to hurry after him.

Alternative Version

If there are more than four performers in the company, the roles of Tom and Blackpool should be played by different actors and Actor 1's speech above should be replaced by the following dialogue:

Louisa I hope, wherever you may go, that you may find greater fortune than you have left behind you in Coketown.

Louisa goes off with Rachael showing her out

Tom (who is present throughout the scene if another actor is available) seems ready to follow them, then, at the last moment turns to Blackpool

Tom I say! I think I may be able to do you a good turn. Don't ask me what it is, because it might come to nothing; but you remember the light porter at the bank?
Blackpool Him as brought me message today?
Tom That's the fellow. Now, when are you off?

Blackpool Well, sir. Monday today. That gives us ... well, it'll be Friday. Friday or Saturday.

Tom Friday or Saturday. Now, look here. When you leave work of a night, between now and when you go away ... just wait around the bank for an hour or so. And if this good turn I can do you should come to anything, the light porter will have a message for you.

Blackpool Light porter. Ay, I'll remember him.

Tom Don't speak to him unless he speaks to you. It might come to nothing, see. Just go to the bank and wait.

Blackpool I understand, sir.

Tom (*smiling*) Good man. (*He calls off*) Loo!! Wait for me, Loo!

Tom goes

Blackpool is now alone on stage, a spotlight on him

Blackpool Hour waiting outside bank yesterday. Hour day before. Today, I finished at me loom, came straight to bank. Waited around. For nowt. Light porter gave us a funny look but said nowt. Old lady at winder stared. Felt tired. Harder work, standing doin' nowt than busy at loom. Nothing. Waited two hour, then gev it up as a bad job. Home. Got packed up. Said me farewells to Rachael. Next morning, early, Stephen Blackpool, walking on road out of Coketown.

Slow fade to Black-out

SCENE 20

The Lights come up on Actress 1

Actress 1 Mr Bounderby had taken possession of a house and grounds, about fifteen miles from the town, and accessible within a mile or two by a railway, striding on many arches over a wild country, undermined by deserted coal-shafts, and spotted at night by fires and black shapes of stationary engines at pits' mouths. This country, gradually softening towards the neighbourhood of Mr Bounderby's retreat, there mellowed into a rustic landscape. It was among the leafy shadows of this retirement in the long, sultry summer days, that Mr Harthouse began to prove the face which had set him wondering when he first saw it, and to try if it would change for him.

More Lights come up. A hot summer's day. Louisa is sitting in a clearing, lost in herself

Harthouse appears

Harthouse Mrs Bounderby.

Louisa starts

I'm so glad I've found you alone. I have for some time had a particular wish to speak to you.

Pause

Your brother, my young friend Tom——

She looks at him with immediate interest. He stops

I am sorry. The expression of your sisterly interest is so . . . beautiful, I am
compelled to stop for a moment and admire.

Louisa I am waiting, Mr Harthouse, for further reference to my brother.

Harthouse How rigid you are with me. But I do deserve it. My subject is not
you, but your brother. I have an interest in him.

Louisa Have you an interest in anything, Mr Harthouse?

Harthouse If you had asked me when I first came here, I should have said
"No". I must now say . . . yes.

Louisa I give you credit for being interested in my brother.

Harthouse You have done much for him. Your whole life, Mrs Bounderby,
expresses such charming self-forgetfulness on his account . . .

Louisa gets up, about to go

Pardon me again, I am running wide of the subject. I am interested in him
for his own sake.

Louisa Please come to the point, Mr Harthouse.

Harthouse A young fellow of your brother's years is often a little . . . the
common phrase is dissipated. Is he?

Louisa Yes, I think he is.

Harthouse Allow me to be frank. Do you think he games at all?

Louisa I think he makes bets.

Pause

I know he makes bets.

Harthouse And of course he loses.

Louisa Yes.

Harthouse Of course. May I hint at the probability of your sometimes
supplying him with money for these purposes.

Louisa looks at him, a little resentful

Mrs Bounderby, I think Tom may be gradually falling into trouble. I wish
to stretch out a helping hand to him. For *his* sake.

Louisa tries to speak, but nothing comes of it

It has occurred to me that Tom has not had many of the advantages of
most young men in his position. For instance, I wonder if it is likely that
any great amount of confidence has been established between Tom and
his father.

Louisa It is . . . not likely, Mr Harthouse.

Harthouse Or between Tom and his brother-in-law?

Louisa I do not think that likely either.

Harthouse Mrs Bounderby. May there be a better confidence between us?
Tom has borrowed a considerable sum of you, has he not?

Pause

Louisa You will understand, Mr Harthouse, that if I answer your question,
I do not do so by way of complaint or regret.

Pause

When I married, I found my brother was, even at that time, heavily in debt. Heavily enough to oblige me to sell some trinkets. They were no sacrifice. I sold them very willingly. They were quite worthless to me.

Pause

Since then, I have given my brother, at various times, what money I could spare. Recently, since you have been in the habit of visiting here, he has wanted in one sum, as much as one hundred pounds. I have not been able to give it to him. I have felt uneasy for the consequences of his being so involved. I have kept this a secret until now.

Harthouse Mrs Bounderby, you can most assuredly trust it to my honour. As to Tom, we have agreed that he has perhaps not been as fortunate in his early training as might have been the case, and an allowance must be made. I have one great fault to find with Tom, however, which I cannot forgive, and for which I take him heavily into account.

Louisa And what fault might that be?

Harthouse I cannot forgive him for not being more sensible, in every word, look and action, of the affection of his best friend; of her unselfishness; of her sacrifice. The return he makes her, within my observation, is a very poor one. Careless fellow as I am, it is not a fault I am prepared to overlook.

Louisa (*emotional*) I pray you, Mr Harthouse, do not go on. I can see Tom coming this way.

Harthouse My hope in this matter, Mrs Bounderby is to correct your brother. To win for you his constant love and gratitude which you have done much to deserve. My better knowledge of his circumstances, and my direction and advice in extricating him, will give me some influence over him, and all I gain I shall certainly use towards this end.

Louisa I thank you, Mr Harthouse for your concern. Please excuse me. I would not wish to see my brother here under these present circumstances.

She moves away

Harthouse moves to one side

Tom comes on

Harthouse Tom!

Tom is startled. He has a disconsolate air

Tom Oh, hello. I didn't know you were here.
Harthouse Tom. I want a word with you.

Tom sits

Tom. You have appeared a little doleful of late. What's the matter?
Tom Oh, I am hard up and bothered out of my life.
Harthouse My good fellow, so am I.
Tom You! You are the picture of independence, Mr Harthouse. I am in a horrible mess. You have no idea what a state I've got myself into. What a state my sister might have got me out of, if she would only have done it.

Harthouse Tom, you are inconsiderate. You expect too much of your sister. You have had money of her, you dog, you know you have.

Tom Well, Mr Harthouse, I know I have. How else was I to get it? What is a fellow to do for money and where am I to look for it if not from my sister?

Harthouse But my dear Tom, if your sister has not got it——

Tom Not got it, Mr Harthouse? I don't say she has got it. But she could get it. You know she didn't marry Old Bounderby for her own sake, or for his sake, but for my sake. Then why doesn't she get what I want, out of him, for my sake? She could coax it out of him if she chose, but no. There she sits in his company like a stone instead of making herself agreeable to him and getting it easily. I don't know what you may call this, but I call it unnatural conduct.

Harthouse My dear Tom, let me try to be your banker.

Tom For God's sake, don't talk about bankers!

Harthouse What is the present need, Tom? Three figures? Out with them. Say what they are.

Tom Mr Harthouse, it is too late. The money is of no use to me at present. I should have had it before, to be of use to me. But I am very much obliged to you; you're a true friend.

Harthouse Well, it may be of more use by and by. And, my good fellow, if you open your bedevilments to me when they come thick upon you, I may show you better ways out of them than you can find for yourself.

Tom (*almost tearful*) Thank you. I wish I had known you sooner.

Harthouse Now, Tom. Every man is selfish in everything he does, and I am exactly like my fellow creatures in that respect. Now, I am desperately intent on you softening towards your sister—which you ought to do; and on being a more loving and agreeable sort of brother—which you ought to be.

Tom I will be, Mr Harthouse.

Harthouse No time like the present, Tom. Begin at once.

Tom Certainly I will. And my sister Loo shall say so.

Harthouse Having made which bargain, Tom, we will tear ourselves asunder until dinner-time.

He goes

Tom sits. He hears something

Tom Loo? Loo?

Louisa is there. She goes towards him

I . . . I didn't mean to be cross, Loo. I know you are fond of me. And you know I am fond of you.

He takes her hand and kisses it. She smiles, then reflects, looks off in the direction where Harthouse has gone

The Lights fade

SCENE 21

Actress 2 And so, next morning, there was a look of interest for Mr

Harthouse from Louisa as he sat down for breakfast. A look sufficiently encouraging to sustain him all day through a meeting connected with the opportunity of going in for the Gradgrind men, conducted at some distance from Coketown. Mr Harthouse being absent at this public occasion, he did not see Mr Bounderby, purple in the face, arriving home from the bank at an unexpectedly early hour.

Bounderby's drawing-room. Louisa is sitting, reading

Bounderby rushes in

Bounderby Louisa. Louisa. Have you heard?

Louisa Heard what?

Bounderby Then you haven't heard. The bank's been robbed.

Louisa Robbed?

Bounderby Robbed last night with a false key.

Louisa No.

Bounderby The fellows must have been surprised. Only got away with a hundred and fifty-odd pound. Out of the little safe in young Tom's closet. But they were within an ace of making off with twenty thousand pound.

Louisa Out of Tom's safe?

Bounderby Twenty thousand? Twice twenty! Yes, out of Tom's safe.

Louisa And . . . where is Tom now?

Bounderby Helping the police at the bank. He won't be back till very late.

Louisa One hundred and fifty?

Bounderby Quite so. If I may say so, Loo, it does you credit to take this news so hard. But bear up! These fellows will be apprehended. We have a suspect already.

Louisa Who?

Bounderby A hand. The fellow who came whining in here because even his own people would have nothing to do with him.

Louisa Not Stephen Blackpool?

Bounderby The same.

Louisa But——

Bounderby Yes, I know. I know all about "but". They are the finest people in the world, those fellows. They are the salt of the earth. But I tell you what. Show me a dissatisfied hand, and I'll show you a man that's fit for anything bad.

Louisa But he seemed——

Bounderby Seemed? I daresay he seemed.

Mrs Sparsit enters, nerves jangling publicly

But here's Mrs Sparsit, who, with her own eyes, saw him loitering in the vicinity of the bank two nights together.

Mrs Sparsit Lurking, Miss Gradgrind—I beg pardon, Mrs Bounderby— lurking after dark, familiarizing himself, in all probability, with the routine of the premises.

Bounderby And there's an old woman in it too. Seems to have been flying into town on a broomstick every now and then. She watches the bank one whole day before Blackpool begins, and then is seen making her report to him.

Louisa An old woman?

Bounderby Indeed so. (*To Mrs Sparsit*) I beg you ma'am, sit down.

He turns Louisa out of her chair. Mrs Sparsit occupies it in triumph

Loo, Mrs Sparsit's nerves have been acted upon by this business, and she'll stay here a day or two, so make her comfortable.

Mrs Sparsit I pray you, do not let my comfort be a consideration. Anything will do for me.

The scene dissolves. A lighting change

Actress 1 It soon appeared that if Mrs Sparsit had a failing in her association with that domestic establishment, it was that she was so excessively regardless of herself and regardful of others as to be a nuisance. But her greatest point, first and last, was her determination to pity Mr Bounderby.

The Lights come up on Bounderby's drawing-room

Mrs Sparsit and Bounderby are playing backgammon. Mrs Sparsit victoriously bears off her last two men. Bounderby sinks back in his chair

Bounderby Well, ma'am. It's a long time since I last played at backgammon. Not since I had the honour of having you live under my roof.

Mrs Sparsit Miss Gradgrind—I beg your pardon, Mrs Bounderby—takes no interest in the game?

Bounderby None at all. But it has diverted me tonight, after the terrible blow I suffered this morning. (*After a pause*) What's the matter, ma'am, what are you staring at? You don't see a fire, do you?

Mrs Sparsit Oh dear no, sir. I was thinking it imprudent of Miss Gradgrind—Mrs Bounderby—to be walking in the night air without a shawl to keep her from the cold. But on closer observation, I perceive she is accompanied by the excellent Mr Harthouse, who can doubtless supervise her protection more zealously than either of us.

Bounderby Quite so, ma'am. Well, there is nothing for me to do now, but to retire to bed with a glass of water.

Mrs Sparsit Water, sir? Not your sherry warm with lemon-peel and nutmeg, that I was wont to make for you? You are losing all your good old habits. If Miss Gradgrind will permit me, I will offer to make it for you as I have often done.

She scuttles off

Bounderby Why ma'am. I am indebted to you. (*Out front*) So Mr Bounderby retired that night with a fortified beverage and a maudlin persuasion that he had been crossed in something tender, though he could not, for his life, have said what it was.

He goes

Louisa comes on. It is much later, dark. She is in her nightgown, holding an oil lamp

Louisa Tom? Tom?

Tom comes in from outside. He looks tired and drawn

Tom Loo. You shouldn't have waited up. I left word I would be very late. It's past midnight.

Louisa Tom. Have you anything to tell me?

Pause

If ever you loved me in your life, and have anything concealed from everyone besides, tell it to me.

Tom I don't know what you mean. Are you dreaming?

Louisa Tom. Tell me the truth.

Tom I don't know what you mean.

Louisa I will not reproach you. I will be compassionate and true to you. You may be certain I will save you at whatever cost. Say only "yes" and I shall understand you.

She waits. Silence

Not a word, Tom?

Tom Loo. I'm tired. Go to bed.

Louisa I'm sorry. Of course you're tired. With all the hurry and disturbances today. Are there any fresh discoveries?

Tom Nothing you haven't heard from—him.

Louisa Tom? Have you told anyone? That we made a visit. To those people. That we saw Blackpool and those two women together.

Tom We agreed to keep it secret.

Louisa But I didn't know then what was going to happen.

Tom Neither did I.

Louisa Perhaps we should tell someone about it now.

Tom Perhaps. Say what you like. It doesn't matter.

Louisa The man I gave the money to. Do you really believe he is implicated?

Tom shrugs

He seemed honest.

Tom I hope he is. I had my doubts at the time. You may remember I took him outside the door. I told him to think himself pretty well off to get such a windfall from my sister.

Louisa Did that ... offend him?

Tom He took it pretty well.

Louisa And you have nothing more to tell me.

Tom Loo, I am so tired, I wonder I don't say anything, just to be rid of you to get to sleep. Go to bed.

She goes to him and kisses him

Louisa Good-night, Tom. And I hope your nights are many, and much happier than this one.

Tom Good-night, Loo.

Louisa goes

Suddenly Tom bows his head. He gives a stifled cry. Some moments. The Lights fade

SCENE 22

General lighting comes up

Actress 1 Mrs Sparsit, lying by to recover the tone of her nerves in Mr Bounderby's retreat, soon insinuated herself into the routine of the household. She usurped Louisa's position as custodian of the breakfast tea-pot, and regularly followed this service with the implanting of a chaste kiss on her benefactor's cheek as he left for the office. But as soon as this morning ritual was completed, Mrs Sparsit scuttled to the library and there, mindful of the growing incompatibility between Mr Bounderby and his wife, addressed her verdict on the subject to the face of her benefactor's portrait.

Mrs Sparsit stares at the portrait

Mrs Sparsit Serves you right, you noodle, and I am glad of it!

Actor 1 Morning after morning, Mrs Sparsit's judgement never wavered.

Mrs Sparsit Noodle! Noodle! Noodle!

Actor 1 But Mr Bounderby, not wishing to be deprived of the quite different sentiments of pity which she habitually addressed to his face, commanded her, even when her prolonged stay at his retreat had come to an end, to spend every weekend in the country as part of the household.

Mrs Sparsit Now, Mrs Sparsit was not a poetical woman; but she took an idea in the nature of an allegorical fancy into her head. She erected in her mind a mighty staircase, with a dark pit of shame and ruin at the bottom; and down those stairs, from day to day and hour to hour, she saw Louisa coming. She would sit in her chamber window, watching Louisa in an alcove in the garden with Mr Harthouse, whispering together, his face almost touching her hair.

We see Harthouse and Louisa seated together, whispering

Night and day, Mrs Sparsit kept her staircase standing, and there Louisa always was, upon it. And always gliding down, down, down!

Louisa glides past Mrs Sparsit, descending slowly

Eager to see it accomplished, and yet patient, she waited for the last fall, as for the ripeness and fullness of the harvest of her hopes.

Actor 1 So the time went on; until it happened that one Friday, Mr Bounderby was called away from home by business for three or four days.

Mrs Sparsit Tom. Mr Harthouse is away, is he not?

Tom Shooting in Yorkshire. Sent Loo a basket half as big as a church.

Mrs Sparsit And when does he return?

Tom Tomorrow. I'm meeting him at the station in the evening, and I'm dining with him afterwards. But he says he won't be coming down to the country house for a week or so, being due somewhere else.

Mrs Sparsit Ah! I wonder, Tom, if you would pass on a message to your respectful sister. Tell her that I will not be troubling her with my society this weekend, my nerves being a little weak.

Tom goes

On the evening of the next day, a Saturday, Mrs Sparsit put on her bonnet and shawl and went quietly out, having her reasons for hovering in a furtive way about the station by which a passenger would arrive from Yorkshire ...

The Company creates the platform of a railway station, with people waiting for a train

... and for preferring to peep into it round pillars and corners and out of ladies' waiting-room windows, to appearing in its precincts openly.

Tom is waiting on the platform. The train comes in. Tom looks up and down the platform. No Harthouse

Tom Confound the man! He must have missed it. I say! How long till the next train from Yorkshire?

The Station-master can be an off-stage voice if necessary

Station-master Hour and forty minutes, sir.

Tom Confound the man!

Mrs Sparsit This is a device to keep him out of the way. Harthouse is with his sister now!

Actor 1 It was the conception of an inspired moment and she shot off with her utmost swiftness to work it out. The station for the country house was at the opposite end of the town, the time was short, the road not easy; but she was so quick in pouncing on a disengaged coach and diving into the train, that she was borne along the arches as if she had been caught up in a cloud and whirled away.

The Lights dim

Mrs Sparsit Gliding out of the carriage, down the wooden steps, across the stone road, into a green lane, approaching the house. No lights. All silent. No-one in the garden. Then she thought of the wood. Low voices close at hand.

Harthouse His voice.

Louisa And hers.

Mrs Sparsit Yes, in the clearing.

Louisa and Harthouse are together. Mrs Sparsit watches. Louisa hangs her head, not looking at him

Harthouse My dearest love, what could I do? Knowing you were alone, was it possible I could stay away?

Louisa Go away, leave me.

Harthouse I cannot. It is impossible. Don't ask me.

Louisa I am not asking. I am commanding.

Harthouse Then I must disobey.

Louisa Leave me.

He puts his arm around her. Mrs Sparsit exults

Rain begins to fall, softly at first

Harthouse Will you not bear with my society for a little while?

Louisa Not here.
Harthouse Where?
Louisa Not here.
Harthouse We have so little time.
Louisa Must I command you again?
Harthouse We must meet, Louisa, where shall we meet?

They both start suddenly at a noise

Louisa There's someone there.
Harthouse No. Rain. Listen. I'll ride up to the house in a few minutes and announce myself.
Louisa No!

He holds her

Harthouse Louisa, how can you be so cruel when——
Louisa No.
Harthouse When I love you so much.

They freeze

Mrs Sparsit His devotion. His adoration. His love. All this and more until he climbed the fence and led his horse away.

Harthouse goes

Leaving Mrs Sparsit unsure where they were to meet or when, except that it was to be this night, and that by tracking Louisa, Mrs Sparsit would be brought to the rendezvous.

Louisa gets up

Louisa Out of the wood. Into the house.
Mrs Sparsit Rain in a sheet of water. My white stockings a blotchy green. Prickly things in my shoes, water cascading from my bonnet, my chin, my nose. What next?
Louisa Out of the house. Cloaked and muffled. Stealing away.
Mrs Sparsit She elopes. Falling from the lowermost stair into the gulf.
Louisa Into the green lane. Across the stone road. Up the wooden steps.
Mrs Sparsit Following at a short distance. Into the green lane. Across the stone road. Up the wooden steps. The rain falling in torrents.
Louisa The station. Waiting for the Coketown train. Thunder and lightning.

Mrs Sparsit pulls her shawl over her bonnet, disguised

Mrs Sparsit The Coketown train. Fire and steam and smoke.
Station-master Coketown train! Coketown train!
Louisa Into a carriage. A hiss of steam, a crash, a bell, the shriek of the engine.
Mrs Sparsit Into the next carriage. The rolling motion. The station a speck in the storm. Where will she meet him? Where will they go? Where will she meet him? Where will they go?
Louisa Train stopping. Streets under water. Gutters bursting, drains overflowing. Out of the carriage.

Station-master Coketown station! Coketown station!

Mrs Sparsit Coketown station. Where will she meet him? How will she go? A coach, surely. Must see the number, hear the order.

Louisa But Louisa got into no coach and was already gone.

Mrs Sparsit Eyes fastened on her carriage. The door still shut. Cautiously up to the carriage. Passing. Re-passing. Looking in. No-one there!

Louisa Running through the streets!

Mrs Sparsit Wet through!

Louisa Running through the streets ...

Mrs Sparsit Feet squelching and squashing ...

Louisa Must see him ...

Mrs Sparsit Through and through ...

Louisa Must see him ...

Mrs Sparsit Every button, string, hook and eye scouring their image in my back ...

Louisa Running towards him ...

Mrs Sparsit Wet through and through ...

Louisa Running towards him ...

Mrs Sparsit I have lost her!!!

Louisa Running towards him. Father!

Gradgrind is there. Mrs Sparsit is gone

Gradgrind Louisa!

We are in Gradgrind's study. Scene 23 follows without a break

SCENE 23

Louisa Father. I want to speak to you.

Gradgrind Louisa. Have you walked here through this storm?

She lets her cloak and hood fall. She stands, ashen

Louisa Yes, I have.

Gradgrind Louisa. Will you tell me what is the matter?

Louisa The matter ... the matter is that you have trained me from the cradle. And I curse the hour in which I was born to such a destiny. You gave me life. And then you took it away. You turned my mind into a trivial, calculating machine and my heart into a wilderness.

Gradgrind Louisa!

Louisa Remember the last time we spoke in this room? I should have said then what I'm saying now. If only you had given me a moment's help. I'm sorry. It isn't your fault. You couldn't nurture in me the things you never nurtured in yourself. But if only you had. Or if you had only neglected me completely. How much happier I would have been today!

Gradgrind What are you saying, Louisa? My system——

Louisa Your system has robbed me. Of the spring and summer of my life. And all for no purpose. Only for the greater desolation of the world. And to enable me to swallow my revulsion for a husband whom I hate.

Gradgrind My child. My poor child.

Louisa I have hungered, Father. For a region where rules and figures and definitions were not quite absolute. I grew up battling every inch of the way. And then I thought: "What does it matter? What does it matter? Life will soon go by. And nothing in life is worth a struggle."

Gradgrind Louisa. You are so young.

Louisa What does it matter? I took him. I never pretended I loved him. We all knew. My only hope . . . lay in being pleasant and useful to Tom. Tom who has been the subject of all the tenderness of my life. And that was a mistake too. But it doesn't matter . . . except . . . that it may dispose you to think more leniently of his errors. I'm not reproaching you . . . I'm not complaining . . .

Gradgrind What do you want of me, child? What can I do?

Louisa I'll tell you. I met a man. Someone quite different. Light, polished, easy. Affecting a low estimate of everything in life, the same low estimate I had formed myself. What does it matter? The point is, Father, he understood me. He read my thoughts, there was . . . an affinity. The only thing that surprised me was that he cared for nothing . . . and yet he seemed to care so much for me.

Gradgrind For you? Louisa!

Louisa He wanted to gain my confidence. He did gain it. I told him . . . everything.

Gradgrind Louisa!

Louisa No, I haven't disgraced you. But if you ask me whether I have loved him, or do love him, I tell you plainly, Father: it may be so. I don't know.

He holds her

Tonight, my husband being away, he appears, declares his love. He expects me, this minute at his hotel. I made a rendezvous. It was the only way I could release myself of his presence. I don't know if I am sorry . . . or ashamed . . . or degraded . . . All I know is that your philosophy and teaching will not save me. Now Father, you have brought me to this. You ask me what you can do? Save me. Save me by some other means.

He tries to hold her, but she falls to the ground

Quick Black-out

END OF BOOK THE SECOND

SCENE 24

Actress 2 Book the Third; "Garnering".

Harthouse's hotel room. Harthouse is pacing up and down

Harthouse Damn the woman! Damn her eyes! To wait, kicking my heels twenty-four hours together for . . . for a slip of a girl. God! I've never been so *bored*. I would rather go in for . . . for crawling across the Sahara Desert on my hands and knees than go in for another day like this. Waiter! There must be some word, some message. Even the hotel menials are in league against me. Waiter! What if she has divulged all to her husband? Bounderby has the advantage over me in point of weight. If anything of a British nature were to come off between us, I would be marked for life.

The Waiter comes on

Waiter Beg your pardon, sir. You're wanted, sir, if you please.

Harthouse Wanted? What do you mean, wanted? Is the building surrounded by constables?

Waiter Wanted by a young lady, sir.

Harthouse A young lady? Then show her in.

The Waiter goes. Sissy comes in

Sissy I speak to Mr Harthouse.

Harthouse is astonished

Harthouse To Mr Harthouse, yes.

Sissy I think you can guess whom I left just now.

Harthouse I have been in the greatest concern and uneasiness during the last four and twenty hours on a lady's account. The hopes I have been encouraged to form that you come from that lady do not deceive me, I trust.

Sissy I left her within the hour.

Harthouse At——?

Sissy At her father's.

Harthouse is flummoxed

You may be sure, sir, you will never see her again as long as you live.

Silence. Harthouse takes a deep breath

Harthouse So startling an announcement, so confidently made, and by such lips, is really disconcerting in the last degree. May I be permitted to enquire if you are charged to convey that information to me in those hopeless words, by the lady of whom we speak?

Sissy I have no charge from her.

Harthouse Excuse my saying, then, that there is yet hope.

Sissy There is not the least hope. The object of my coming here, sir, is to assure you that you must believe that there is no more hope of your ever speaking with her again than there would be if she had died when she came home last night.

Harthouse Must believe? But if I can't, or won't——
Sissy There is no hope.

Harthouse smiles incredulously. Some moments

Harthouse But you said you had no commission from her.
Sissy I have only the commission of my love for her, and her love for me, a
love of many years' standing, subdued since her marriage, but re-
awakened this morning by her need for a confidante in her hour of crisis. I
have been with her since she came home. I have no further trust than that
I know something of her character and her marriage. Mr Harthouse, I
think you had that trust too.
Harthouse I am not a moral sort of fellow. I am as immoral as need be. At
the same time, in bringing any distress upon the lady who is the subject of
the present conversation, I beg to be allowed to assure you, that I have
had no particularly evil intentions, but have glided on from one step to
another with a smoothness so perfectly diabolical, that I had not the
slightest idea the catalogue was half so long until I began to turn it over.
Whereas I find that it is really in several volumes.

Pause

After what has now been said to me, it seems I have no alternative but to
accept the fact that I shall see this lady no more. I am solely to blame for
the thing having come to this.
Sissy Mr Harthouse. The only reparation that remains with you is to leave
here immediately and finally. I ask you to depart from this place tonight,
under an obligation never to return to it.
Harthouse Look here, do you know the extent of what you ask? You
probably are not aware that I am here on a public kind of business,
preposterous enough in itself, but which I have gone in for, and sworn by,
and am supposed to be devoted to in quite a desperate manner. You
probably are not aware of that, but I assure you, it's the fact.

Sissy looks at him

Besides which, it's so alarmingly absurd, after going in for these fellows,
to back out in such an incomprehensible way.
Sissy I am quite sure, sir, that it is the only reparation in your power. I am
quite sure, or I would not have come here.
Harthouse Upon my soul. I don't know what to say. So ridiculously absurd.
But I see no way out of it. What will be, will be. *This* will be, I suppose. I
must take myself off, I imagine ... in short, I engage to do it.

Sissy moves to go, her mission accomplished

You will permit me to say, that I doubt if any other ambassador or
ambassadress, could have addressed me with the same success. Will you
allow me the privilege of remembering my enemy's name?
Sissy My name?
Harthouse The only name I could possibly care to know tonight.
Sissy Sissy Jupe.
Harthouse Pardon my curiosity at parting? Related to the family?
Sissy I am only a poor girl. I was separated from my father—he was only a

stroller—and taken pity on by Mr Gradgrind. I have lived with the family ever since. Good-night, Mr Harthouse.

Sissy goes

Harthouse Only a poor girl! Only a stroller's daughter! Only James Harthouse made nothing of! Only James Harthouse—a Great Pyramid of failure! (*He kicks the chair*) Waiter!

The Waiter returns

Waiter Sir.
Harthouse Send my fellow here.
Waiter Gone to bed, sir.
Harthouse Well get him up then. And tell him to pack.
Waiter Sir. (*He is about to go*)
Harthouse And take a telegram.

The Waiter takes out pencil and notebook

To the Right Honourable John Harthouse, House of Commons, Westminster, London. Dear Jack. All up at Coketown. Bored out of the place, and going in for—(*pause*)—camels.
Waiter Camels, sir?
Harthouse Yes, blockhead. Camels and be damned.

Quick Black-out

SCENE 25

Actress 1 The indefatigable Mrs Sparsit, with a violent cold upon her, her voice reduced to a whisper, and her stately frame so racked by continual sneezes that it seemed in danger of dismemberment, gave chase to her patron until she found him in the metropolis; and there, majestically sweeping in upon him at his hotel, exploded the combustibles with which she was charged, and blew up. Having executed her mission with infinite relish, this high-minded woman then fainted away on Mr Bounderby's coat-collar.
Actor 1 Mr Bounderby then administered to her by screwing up her thumbs, smiting her hands, abundantly watering her face and inserting salt in her mouth. When these attentions had recovered her, which they very speedily did, Mr Bounderby hustled her into a fast train, and carried her back to Coketown more dead than alive. Utterly heedless of the wear and tear on her clothes and her constitution, and adamant to her pathetic sneezes, Mr Bounderby immediately carried her into a coach, and bore her off to Stone Lodge.

Immediately, Actor 1 and Actress 1 become the characters. Bounderby propels Mrs Sparsit into Gradgrind's study

Bounderby Now, Tom Gradgrind. Here's Mrs Sparsit who has something to say that will strike you dumb.
Gradgrind You have missed my letter.

Bounderby Missed your letter, sir! The present time is no time for letters!

Gradgrind Bounderby. I speak of a very special letter I have written to you, in reference to Louisa.

Bounderby Tom Gradgrind, I speak of a very special messenger that has come to me in reference to Louisa. Mrs Sparsit, ma'am, stand forward.

She does so. She opens her mouth to speak. But no sound comes out. Pause. The men look at her

Mrs Sparsit (*eventually*) I ... I ... Mr Gradgrind ... if you please ... I can't ...

She points to her throat. Bounderby shakes her, but to no avail

Bounderby Mrs Sparsit, this is no time for a lady, however highly connected to be totally inaudible and seemingly swallowing marbles. Tom Gradgrind, Mrs Sparsit lately found herself, by accident, in a situation to overhear a conversation between your daughter and your precious gentleman friend, Mr James Harthouse.

Gradgrind Indeed?

Bounderby Indeed. And in that conversation——

Gradgrind It is not necessary to repeat its tenor, Bounderby. I know what passed.

Bounderby You do? Do you know where your daughter is at the present time?

Gradgrind Undoubtedly. She is here.

Bounderby Here?

Gradgrind Here. The moment she could detach herself from the interview with the person of whom you speak, Louisa hurried here for protection in a state of distraction. She has remained here ever since.

Silence. Bounderby is deflated. He turns on Mrs Sparsit

Bounderby Now, ma'am. We shall be happy to hear any apology you may think proper to offer, for going about the country at express pace, with no other luggage than a Cock and Bull!

Mrs Sparsit (*whispering*) Sir, my nerves are at present too much shaken and my health is at present too much impaired in your service to admit of doing more than taking refuge in tears. (*Which she does*).

Bounderby Well, ma'am, there is something else in which you may take refuge, namely a coach. And the coach in which we came here being at the door, you'll allow me to hand you down to it.

He begins to manhandle her towards the door

Mrs Sparsit I pray you not to trouble yourself on my account. I'll see myself to the coach. Good day, gentlemen.

She goes

Bounderby glares at Gradgrind

Bounderby Well?

Pause

Gradgrind My dear Bounderby——

Bounderby Don't my dear me.

Gradgrind We are all liable to mistakes——

Bounderby What do you mean by "we".

Gradgrind I then. In the course of a few hours, I have become better informed as to Louisa's character than in previous years. The enlightenment has been forced upon me and the discovery is not mine. (*With difficulty*) I think there are qualities in Louisa which have been harshly neglected, and ... a little perverted. And I would suggest to you that— that if you would kindly meet me in a timely endeavour to leave her to her better nature for a while—and to encourage it to develop itself by tenderness and consideration—it ... it would be better for the happiness of all of us. Louisa ... I have always ... been very fond of Louisa ...

Bounderby Are you saying you'd like to keep her here for a time?

Gradgrind I am. She can remain here on a ... visit and be attended by Sissy Jupe who understands her and in whom she trusts.

Bounderby I gather from all this, Tom Gradgrind, that you are of the opinion that there is what people call incompatibility between Loo Bounderby and myself.

Gradgrind I fear there is at present a general incompatibility between Louisa, and—and—almost all the relations in which I have placed her.

Bounderby stands with his legs wide apart, hands in pockets

Bounderby Now look you here, Tom Gradgrind. You have had your say, and I am going to have mine. I am a Coketown man. I am Josiah Bounderby of Coketown. When a man talks to me about imaginative qualities, I always tell that man, whoever he is, that I know what he means. He means turtle soup and venison with a gold spoon, and that he wants to be set up with a coach and six. That's what your daughter wants. Since you are of the opinion that she ought to have what she wants, I recommend you to provide it for her. Because, Tom Gradgrind, she will never have it from me.

Gradgrind Bounderby, I hoped after my entreaty you would have taken a different tone.

Bounderby Incompatibility? Yes, I believe there *is* incompatibility between your daughter and me, and it is to be summed up in this: that your daughter don't properly know her husband's merits, and is not impressed with such a sense as would become her, by George, of the honour of his alliance. That's plain speaking, I hope.

Gradgrind Bounderby, the less we say tonight, the better I think.

Bounderby On the contrary, Tom Gradgrind, the more we say tonight the better, I think. That is till I have said all I mean to say, and then I don't care how soon we stop. I come to a question that may shorten the business. What do you mean by the proposal you made just now?

Gradgrind I mean that I hope you may be induced to arrange, in a friendly manner, for allowing Louisa a period of repose and reflection here which may tend to a gradual alteration for the better in many respects. You have accepted a great charge of her; for better for worse, for——

Bounderby I know what I took her for. As well as you do——

Gradgrind I was merely going on to remark, Bounderby, that we may all be more or less in the wrong, not excepting you; and that some yielding on your part may not only be an act of true kindness, but perhaps a debt incurred towards Louisa.

Bounderby Well I think differently, and I am going to finish this business according to my opinions. I don't want to make a quarrel of it. I don't think it would be worthy of my reputation to make a quarrel of such a subject. If your daughter don't come home tomorrow by twelve o'clock at noon, I shall understand that she prefers to stay away, and I shall send her wearing apparel and so forth over here, and you'll take charge of her for the future.

Gradgrind Let me seriously entreat you to reconsider this, Bounderby, before you commit yourself to such a decision.

Bounderby throws his hat on

Bounderby I will listen to no more sentimental humbug. I have given you my decision and I have got no more to say. Good-night!

The Lights change

Actor 1 So Mr Bounderby went home to his town house to bed. At five minutes past twelve o'clock the next day, he directed Mrs Bounderby's property to be carefully packed up and sent to Tom Gradgrind's; advertised his country retreat for sale by private contract; and resumed a bachelor life.

SCENE 26

A Coketown street. Evening

Actress 1 Rachael, walking home from work.

Rachael comes on. She stares at something ahead of her

Rachael Another placard. Nobbut a wall in Coketown as hasn't had one posted on it. Bounderby's work. (*She reads it*) "A reward of Twenty Pounds is offered for the ... apprehension of Stephen Blackpool, lately a hand at Bounderby's factory, in connection with the bank robbery on the fourteenth day of August this year. Blackpool is aged some forty years, but his appearance suggests a man in his middle fifties ..." The goodest lad, the truest, posted a common criminal.

Louisa comes in on Gradgrind's arm. She is obviously unwell, out for the first time since her flight from Harthouse. She sees Rachael and starts

Louisa Rachael.
Rachael Oh. You. Yo' can show yo'self now then, can yo'?
Gradgrind Louisa?
Louisa This is the woman, Father.
Rachael Ay, this is the woman. (*She points at the placard*) And that there's the man. Stephen Blackpool. The thief. For aw' t' see.
Gradgrind I'll be obliged if you address my daughter with a deal less spleen——

Rachael I'll address as I like them as 'as tekken away my Stephen's good
name.
Gradgrind With a good deal less——
Louisa No Father. The misunderstanding is natural. Rachael, I have seen
you once before.
Rachael Ay, once.
Louisa I was coming, with my father here, to see you again. I have heard
that my ... husband, interviewing you in connection with the robbery,
cast doubt on our interview taking place. I wanted to set the matter right,
with my father as witness. Well, Father, this is the woman in whose
company I saw Stephen Blackpool on the night of which I have spoken.
She saw me giving him two pounds in gold.
Rachael Lending it were, not giving. And he wouldn't tek a bank note.
Louisa That's right. So. Father. If you will be pleased to inform my
husband that this woman is above suspicion——
Rachael I wonder you're not able to inform him yo'self——
Gradgrind My daughter is at present unwell and staying at her old home. It
is at some cost to her personal comfort that she has insisted on seeking
you out tonight.

Pause

Rachael Well, I'll thank you for your trouble. But I can't say what you may
ha' done. The likes of you don't know us. Don't care for us. Don't belong
to us. I can't yet say I'm sure why yo' come to us that night. I can't tell but
what yo' come wi' some aim of your own, not mindin' what hurt yo' did
to poor lad. I said then, bless yo' for comin' and I say it again now. Yo'
seem to have some pity for 'im. But I don't know. I don't know.
Louisa Rachael. You will not mistrust me one day, when you know me
better.
Rachael Happen. Anyroad, the lad'll be back to speak for hi'self soon
enough. Oh ay, I've had word from him. A working colony sixty mile off.
And I've wrote to him today. How he's suspected. He'll be back, straight
off, to clear his good name.
Gradgrind Perhaps you should have surrendered his new address to the
authorities——
Bounderby I'll not have him brought back. When he hears, he'll come of his
own free will. Ay, that'll show him innocent enough, or should do.
Gradgrind He was seen near the bank before it was broken into.
Rachael I can't guess. I can't guess whatever took him there. Makes yo'
wonder what other folk have put him up to.
Gradgrind I think, Louisa, in the best interests of your health, we should
return home as soon as——
Louisa Just one word, Father. The old woman. Who was with you that
night. She, too, is spoken of in this business. Could she not shed some
light on this question?
Rachael The only time I ever saw her. And Stephen saw her but once before
that. But there's no more harm in her than there is in my Stephen. (*She
pauses*) You could let him alone, eh? All on you! (*She looks at them*)

The Lights fade quickly, then come up immediately

SCENE 27

Actress 1 But two days went by, and Rachael received no answer to her letter. Fearing it had gone astray, she gave Stephen's new address to the authorities.

Actor 1 Messengers were sent to the working colony. Rachael's letter had indeed reached Stephen. And he had decamped in the same hour.

Actress 2 Opinion in Coketown was divided as to whether Rachael had written in good faith, or whether she had warned Blackpool to fly.

Actor 1 Was Blackpool the thief?

Actress 2 If not where was the man?

Actress 1 And why did he not come back?

Actor 2 Gradgrind, on his way to discuss these questions with Bounderby, was astonished to see, outside that gentleman's steps, a matron of classical deportment, seizing an ancient woman by the throat, dragging her out of a coach and into Bounderby's house.

Mrs Sparsit drags Mrs Pegler across the stage and into Bounderby's drawing-room

Mrs Sparsit Leave her alone. Let nobody touch her. She belongs to me. It's providence, come inside, ma'am.

Gradgrind Mrs Sparsit, upon my soul!

Mrs Sparsit You here too, sir. Come inside. (*She calls out*) Mr Bounderby! Mr Bounderby, come at once sir!

Mrs Pegler No! Please no!

Gradgrind Mrs Sparsit, who is that lady you are handling with such vigour?

Mrs Sparsit Why, Mr Gradgrind, this is the old woman.

Gradgrind Old woman?

Mrs Sparsit The old woman in the bank robbery.

Mrs Pegler Don't call him! Please don't call him.

Bounderby comes in

Mrs Sparsit My benefactor! Here is the prize I have won you!

Silence. Bounderby stares incredulously at Mrs Pegler

Bounderby Mrs Sparsit, ma'am. What do you mean by this?

Mrs Sparsit It has not been, sir, without some trouble that I have effected this; but trouble in your service is to me a pleasure, and hunger, thirst and cold a real gratification.

Bounderby I ask you again, Mrs Sparsit, what do you mean by this?

Mrs Sparsit Sir?

Bounderby Why don't you mind your own business, ma'am? How dare you go and poke your officious nose into my family affairs?

Mrs Sparsit grates her mittens together in agitation

Mrs Sparsit Sir, you do not seem to realize. This is the woman I saw watching the bank, the one who is in league with Blackpool.

Mrs Pegler My dear Josiah! I am not to blame. I told this lady over and over again, that I knew what she was doing would not be agreeable to you, but she *would* do it.

Bounderby What did you let her bring you for? Couldn't you have knocked her cap off, or scratched her eyes or dislodged a tooth or two?

Mrs Pegler She threatened me that if I resisted her, I should be brought by constables, and it was better to come quietly than make that stir in such a ... (*looking round*) ... fine house as this. I have always lived quietly, Josiah, I have never broken the condition once. I have never said I was your mother.

Stunned reactions

I have come to town sometimes, just to take a proud peep at you. I have done it unbeknown, my love, and gone away.

Bounderby is pacing, discomforted

Gradgrind I am surprised, madam, that in your old age you have the face to claim Mr Bounderby for your son after your unnatural and inhuman treatment of him.

Mrs Pegler Me unnatural? Me inhuman to my dear boy?

Gradgrind Dear? Yes, dear in his self-made prosperity, madam, I dare say. Not very dear however, when you deserted him in his infancy and left him to the brutality of a drunken grandmother.

Mrs Pegler I deserted my Josiah! Now, Lord forgive you, sir, for your wicked imaginations and for your scandal against the memory of my poor mother who died in my arms before Josiah was born. May you repent of it, sir, and live to know better!

Gradgrind Do you deny, then, madam, that you left your son to be—to be brought up in the gutter.

Mrs Pegler Josiah in the gutter! No such thing, sir. Never! For shame on you! My dear boy knows, that though he come of humble parents, and though his poor father died when he were eight year old, he was put prentice to a kind master and worked his way forward to be rich and thriving. And *I'll* give you to know, sir—for my dear boy won't—that though his mother kept but a little village shop, he never forgot her, but pensioned me on *thirty pound a year*, only making the condition that I was to keep down in my own part, which is right, for I should do many unbefitting things up here! I can keep my pride in Josiah to myself and love for love's own sake. And shame on you, sir, to accuse me of being a bad mother to my son, with my son standing here to tell you different!

Silence. Everyone looks at Bounderby

Bounderby Well. I don't know what you're all waiting for. I'm not bound to deliver a lecture on my family affairs. I have not undertaken to do it, and I'm not a-going to do it! So, Tom Gradgrind, if you expect any explanation whatever upon that branch of the subject, I'm afraid you will be disappointed. In reference to the bank robbery, there has been a mistake made concerning my—(*he pauses*)—mother. If there hadn't been over-officiousness, it wouldn't have been made. (*To Mrs Pegler*) Ma'am, you may spend the night here.

Thrilled, she kisses Bounderby and goes off with a helping hand from her son

Mr Gradgrind, goodday to you.

Gradgrind goes

Bounderby turns vengefully on the remaining figure

Mrs Sparsit. I rather think you are cramped here, do you know? It appears to me that under my humble roof there's hardly opening enough for a lady of your genius in other people's affairs.

Mrs Sparsit Really, sir?

Bounderby It appears to me, ma'am, that a different sort of establishment altogether would bring out a lady of *your* powers. Such an establishment as your relation Lady Scadgers maintains. Don't you think you might find some affairs there, ma'am, to interfere with?

Mrs Sparsit It never occurred to me before, sir. But now you mention it, I think it highly probable.

Bounderby Then suppose you try it. I really ought to apologize to you, ma'am, for having stood in your light so long!

Mrs Sparsit Pray don't name it, sir. If your portrait could speak—but it has advantage over the original of not possessing the power of committing itself and disgusting others—it would testify that a long period has elapsed since I first habitually addressed it as the picture of a noodle. Nothing that a noodle does can awaken surprise or indignation: the proceedings of a noodle can only inspire contempt.

She sweeps disdainfully past him and out

Actor 1 (*out front*) But though Bounderby carried it off in these terms, there was a blustering sheepishness about him. Detected as the bully of humility who had built his windy reputation on lies, he cut a most ridiculous figure. Even that unlucky female Mrs Sparsit, was not in so bad a plight as that remarkable man and self-made humbug, Josiah Bounderby of Coketown.

Black-out

In the darkness, we hear voices

Scene 28

Actress 2 Another night.
Actor 1 Another day and night.
Actress 1 And another.
Actress 2 No Stephen Blackpool.
Actor 1 Where was the man?
Actress 1 And why did he not come back?

A faint light comes up on Stephen Blackpool's face. He is lying in the Old Hell Shaft, one arm twisted under his body. He looks up at the sky

Voices Where is the man? Why does he not come back?
Blackpool The Old Hell Shaft. Three days. The Old Hell Shaft. I've heard pitmen say . . . as how it's cursed, this shaft. Folk disappear. Score upon score. Earth gives way. Swallows up. Never seen. Dangerous country. Mad. Mad to cross it at night. Had to. Get to Bounderby. Country house. Face him. Clear me name. Too impatient. Rachael's letter. Rachael. How much longer? Another night coming. Star's out. The one star I can see. Out again. Another night. How long? How long?
Voices Where is the man? Why does he not come back?

Actress 2 (*breaking through the other voices*) There's a man. Old Hell Shaft. Fallen.
Actor 1 There's a man. Fallen down the Old Hell Shaft.
Actress 1 Dangerous country.
Actress 2 They found his hat.
Actor 1 Swallowed up.
Actress 1 Bring candles.
Actress 2 Bring ropes.
Actor 1 A windlass.
Actress 1 Stephen Blackpool!
Actress 2 The Old Hell Shaft.
Actor 1 Quick!
Actress 1 Stephen Blackpool's fallen down the Old Hell Shaft!
Actress 2 Fetch a doctor!
Blackpool How long? How long? The star, the star.

All except the Blackpool actor go to the opposite side of the stage, holding a long rope. Light from lanterns. Two actors pay out the rope slowly. The third pulls on the end of the rope, moving with difficulty "downwards", i.e. across the stage towards Blackpool

Rescuer More rope! Keep lowering!
Voice More rope! Keep lowering!

The Rescuer eventually reaches Blackpool and fastens the rope around him

Rescuer Haul away!
Haulers Heave! Heave!

The rope is pulled in. Blackpool and the Rescuer reach the "safe" side of the stage. During the following, Blackpool is eased on to a makeshift stretcher

Hauler Alive or dead?
Rescuer Alive, but he's hurt bad.

Rachael comes forward

Rachael Stephen.
Blackpool Rachael. Rachael, my dear.

She takes his hand

Don't let go.
Rachael I'll not. You're in pain, Stephen.
Blackpool Not now. Have been. But that's over now.
Rachael Stephen.
Blackpool You know, Rachael, I remember reading petition. Sent round by pitmen. About this shaft. Petitioning pit-owners to make safe all the worked-out holes in't' ground. I remember how it went, it went: "When shaft were in work, it killed wi'out need: when 'tis let alone, it kills wi'out need." Stuck in me mind. I never signed it. They passed it round and I never signed it.
Rachael Never fret over that now, Stephen.
Blackpool Muddled. I've been muddled all life through. That's what happened 'tween me and t'other hands. Between me and Mr Bounderby.

Hadn't been for that, I'd never have been making my way across top of shaft at dead of night to see Bounderby.

Rachael That's past, Stephen. Yo' must speak out now, clear yo' name. Bounderby's here. Whole town's been looking for yo'. Ay and half of them have turned out to rescue yo'.

Louisa comes on

Blackpool Is that young lady?

Louisa It's me. (*She pauses*) My brother. What did he say? That night when he spoke to you alone?

Blackpool He said how if I was to wait around bank next few nights, it might be to my advantage. So. Question him. I mek no charges. But ask him.

Louisa nods

I were angry wi' you. I thought it were all one, what yo' brother had said to me, what yo' had said to me. I thought it were a plot between two on you. I must say sorry to yo' for thinkin' ill o' yo' kindness.

Louisa squeezes his hand, then retreats into the darkness

Rachael, see that star? Three nights I've watched it. It's been my comfort and my only light. It's been my faith in God. And my hope as somehow, there might be a way through t'muddle. I can't see t'road. But there's others might. The star, Rachael, the star. Don't let go my hand. We may walk together tonight, any road.

Rachael Ay. We may that.

Blackpool The star ... the star ...

Rachael lets his hand drop

Rachael Very few whispers broke the silence. It was soon a funeral procession.

Slow fade to Black-out. The Lights come up almost immediately

Scene 29

Actor 2 Before the ring of people round the Old Hell Shaft had dispersed, one figure had disappeared from within it. Tom had not stood near Louisa, but in a retired place by himself. When Louisa was speaking to Blackpool, Sissy, attentive to all that happened, slipped towards Tom and whispered in his ear. Without turning his head, he conferred with her for a few moments, and vanished. Thus the whelp had gone out of the circle before the people moved. Tom did not come home that night, nor, when his father looked, was he at his place in the bank the next morning.

The Lights change. The drawing-room at Stone Lodge. Gradgrind stands in thought

Gradgrind Louisa! Sissy!

They come on

What did Blackpool say to you last night about the robbery?

Louisa He told me to question Tom about it and ...

Gradgrind Yes?

Louisa He told me it was Tom who made him wait at the bank for those three evenings.

Gradgrind Too plain. It is too plain.

Louisa I fear so Father, I know he needed money.

Gradgrind And Blackpool being about to leave town, it served Tom's purpose to cast suspicion upon him.

Louisa It must have flashed into his mind while we sat there, Father. The visit to Blackpool's lodgings was my idea.

Gradgrind And now, how is he to be found? How is he to be saved from justice? In the few hours that can possibly elapse before I publish the truth, how is he to be found by us, and only by us? Ten thousand pounds could not effect it.

Louisa Sissy has effected it, Father.

Gradgrind turns to Sissy

Gradgrind It is always you, my child.

Sissy We had our fears before yesterday. Then, when I saw Louisa speaking to Blackpool last night, I went to Tom when no-one saw and told him to escape at once for his father's sake and his own. He didn't know where to go. He had little money and could think of no-one who might hide him. I thought of Father's old circus. I have not forgotten where Mr Sleary goes at this time of the year. I told Tom to hurry there and tell his name and ask Mr Sleary to hide him till I came. Then he shrank away among the people.

Gradgrind And where is Sleary's troupe playing at present?

Sissy A town not far from Liverpool. So he may be got to the port and spirited away to any part of the world.

Gradgrind Then we must act with speed. Louisa, you and Sissy will travel together by a circuitous course. I will travel alone, setting off in the opposite direction to you, and arriving by a wider route. By this means, we will deter any suspicious persons from guessing at our aim.

Gradgrind goes

A lighting change. Sissy and Louisa tell the story with mounting excitement

Sissy Sissy and Louisa travelled by night ...

Louisa Were turned out at a swamp just after dawn, a mile or two from the town they sought ...

Sissy And were rescued from this dismal spot by a savage old postillion, kicking a horse in a fly ...

Louisa And so were smuggled into the town by all the back lanes where the pigs lived, and at one o'clock stopped in the market place ...

Sissy Where stood a familiar canvas-sided apartment.

A moment of jubilation as Sleary comes towards them holding a glass of brandy and water

Sleary Thethilia, it doth me good to thee you!!!

Sissy Mr Sleary!!!

They embrace. Sleary looks at Louisa

Sleary And thith, I take it, ith Mith Thquire! (*He beams at Louisa*)
Sissy Tom's sister, yes.
Sleary I hope I thee you well, mith, and I hope the Thquire'th well.
Louisa My father will be here soon. Is my brother safe?
Sleary Thafe and thound. Take a peep at the ring, mith, through here.

They look through a spy-hole in the tent

Thath Jack the Giant Killer—piethe of comic infant bithnith. The clown
with a thaucepan lid and a thpit ith Jackth thervant; therth little Jack in a
thplendid thuit of armour: two comic black thervanth; and the Giant——

They look up higher

—whoth jutht been killed.

They look at the ground

You thee them all?
Louisa Yes, but——
Sleary I have my opinionth and the Thquire hath hith. I don't want to
know what your brotherth been up to; and ith better for me not to know.
All I thay ith, the Thquire hath thtood by Thethilia and I'll thtand by the
Thquire. Your brother ith one of them black thervanth!

Exclamations of surprise

Ith a fact, and even knowing it, you couldn't put your finger on it. The
performanth hath jutht finithhed. I'll send him through.

Sleary goes off towards the ring, applauding

Louisa He will not speak to me.
Sissy He must. Louisa, if your husband has discovered the truth, he will
have men searching for Tom everywhere. I'll find out the quickest way of
getting him to Liverpool.

She rushes off

*Tom comes on wiping off his make-up with a towel. He sees Louisa, stops
still*

Louisa Tom!

Pause

Sissy and I have travelled all night. We are here to help you.
Tom Sleary said there was a friend to see me.
Louisa Tom. I above all others have always been your friend.

Pause

Tom. Tell me the truth. How was it done?
Tom How was what done?
Louisa The robbery.

Pause

Tom I forced the safe overnight and shut it up ajar before I went away. I had had the key that was found made long before. I dropped it that morning that it might be supposed to have been used. I didn't take the money all at once. I pretended to put my balance away every night, but I didn't. Now you know all about it.

Louisa I still can't believe it of you, Tom.

Tom I don't see why. So many people are employed in situations of trust; so many people out of so many will be dishonest. We have heard Father talk a hundred times of its being a law. How can I help laws?

Louisa Tom. Listen to me. Atone by repentence and better conduct for the shocking act you have committed and the dreadful consequences to which it has led. Now kiss me, Tom, and may God forgive you as I do.

Tom No. I don't want anything to do with you.

Louisa Tom. Do we end so after all my love?

Tom Love! A pretty love, flouncing out on Old Bounderby, packing off my good friend Mr Harthouse and going home just when I was in the greatest danger. Pretty love that! Clearing the woman Rachael from suspicion. Pretty love that! You have regularly given me up! You never cared for me.

Sissy rushes on

Sissy Quickly, Tom. Your father has just arrived. He has some money for you. And Mr Sleary has a new disguise. Hurry!

Tom rushes off

Louisa After all my love for him, he can scarcely bear to look at me.

Sissy Quickly, Louisa. It's over ten miles to the railway. There's a coach in half an hour that catches the mail train to Liverpool. We must get one of the horse riders to take Tom to the coach.

Louisa He will go to Liverpool, get a ship abroad and I will never see him again.

Sissy Louisa! We must find a way of getting Tom to the coach now!

Bitzer comes on, breathless and steaming

Bitzer I'm sorry to interfere with your plans——

Sissy Bitzer!

Bitzer Very sorry indeed. But I can't allow myself to be outdone by a pack of horseriders. I am taking young Tom away.

Sissy You're too late. We have smuggled him out of here.

Bitzer Oh no, miss. Oh no. It is you who are too late. I have two fine sturdy fellows who have even now arrested young Tom, and will take him back to justice under my supervision.

Gradgrind rushes in

Gradgrind Bitzer! Is it you who have engineered my son's arrest?

Bitzer knuckles away

Bitzer Indeed it is, sir. There have been few clues, but I have pursued them all diligently.

Gradgrind Bitzer, have you a heart?

Bitzer The circulation of the blood, sir, couldn't be carried on without one. No man, sir, acquainted with the facts established by Harvey relating to the circulation of the blood, can doubt I have a heart.

Gradgrind Is it accessible to any compassionate influence?

Bitzer It is accessible to reason, sir, and to nothing else.

Gradgrind What motive can you have for preventing the escape of this wretched youth and crushing his miserable father? See his sister here. Pity us!

Bitzer Sir, I have suspected young Tom of this bank robbery from the first. I had had my eye on him before that time, for I knew his ways. I have kept my observations to myself, but I have made them and I have got ample proofs against him. I am going to take Mr Tom back to Coketown in order to deliver him to Mr Bounderby. Sir, I have no doubt whatever that Mr Bounderby will then promote me to young Tom's situation. And I wish to have his situation, sir, for it will be a rise to me and will do me good.

Gradgrind If this is solely a question of self-interest with you——

Bitzer I beg your pardon for interrupting you, sir, but I am sure you know that the whole social system is a question of self-interest. What you must appeal to is a person's self-interest. It's your only hold. We are so constituted. I was brought up in that catechism when I was very young, sir, as you are aware.

Gradgrind What sum of money will you set against your expected promotion?

Bitzer Thank you, sir, for hinting at the proposal; but I will not set any sum against it. Knowing that your clear head would propose that alternative, I have gone over the calculations in my mind; and I find that to compound a felony, even on very high terms indeed, would not be as safe and as good for me as my improved prospects at the bank. Sir.

Gradgrind Bitzer! Bitzer! You were many years at my school. If, in remembrance of the pains bestowed upon you there, you can persuade yourself to disregard your present interest and release my son, I entreat and pray you to give him the benefit of that remembrance.

Bitzer I really wonder sir, to find you taking a position so untenable. My schooling was paid for; it was a bargain; and when I came away the bargain ended. I don't deny that my schooling was cheap. But that comes right, sir. I was made in the cheapest market and have to dipose myself in the dearest. If you will excuse me, sir, I will take my prisoner to justice.

Bitzer goes off

Gradgrind, Louisa and Sissy look at one another. The following section is played out front

Louisa Tired and dirty from travel, downcast at the failure of our desperate expedition and fearful for Tom's future, we could do little but watch . . .

Gradgrind As Bitzer instructed his two underlings to convey their wretched charge away in a horse and cart . . .

Sissy While even Mr Sleary, apparently deciding that Tom's offence was no small thing, seemed content to abet the expedition with the loan of a couple of outriders.

Louisa The small procession disappeared from view . . .

Gradgrind Leaving us to recover ourselves as best we could by finding a nearby hostelry . . .

Sissy Where we spent a disconsolate night. By eight o'clock the next morning, we were ready to return to Coketown.

Sleary comes on, apparently downcast

Sleary Thquire. Thithy. Mith Thquire. The young Thquire ith at thith moment on hith way to . . . (*suddenly euphoric*) America!!!!

All are elated. Sissy hugs Sleary

Gradgrind What! But . . . we saw you packing him back to Coketown with Bitzer.

Sleary A prethiouth rathcal! All I thay ith thith; you thtood by Thethilia, Thquire, tho I thtood by you! I had two of my men, Childerth and Gordon, riding with them, ath ith to thow the way. I followed with my dog in a horth and cart. I'd tipped young Tom off before we left, tho he wath prepared. Thoon ath I came up behind, Childerth and Gordon rode up alongthide of Bither'th cart and forthed the cart over on ith thide into the ditch. They took care of the two guardth, my dog grabbed Bither by the throat and thoon, young Tom wath in my cart heading back by a different route. Well, my horth can do fifteen mile an hour, and my dog can pin a man to the thpot for twenty-four hourth. After hith two hire-lingth had run away, Bither had no cardth left to play. The dog thtill had him on the ground at four o'clock thith morning, when I thent word that Tom wath thafely away. I ecthpect he'th walking back to Coketown now!

Sissy (*hugging him*) Mr Sleary!

Sleary Thethilia, it wath no trouble at all.

Gradgrind Mr Sleary, it is impossible for me to thank you adequately for this service. But if there is any remuneration I can make . . .

Sleary I don't want money mythelf, Thquire, but Childerth and Gordon are both family men, tho a five pound note each might be accthetable. Likewise, if you want to thtand a collar for the dog and a thet of bellth for the horth, I thould be very glad to take 'em. Brandy and water I alwayth take. And if you don't think it going too far, a thpread for the company at three and thix a head would make 'em happy.

Gradgrind Mr Sleary, I am more than willing to stand all these small expenses, though they seem slight payment for what you have effected.

Sleary Thquire, if you'll only give the Horth-riding a bethpeak whenever you can, you'll more than balanthe the account. Now, Thquire, if your daughter and Thithy will excuthe me, I thould like one parting word with you.

Louisa and Sissy go

Gradgrind And what, Mr Sleary, is the subject of this . . . word?

Sleary Dogth, Thquire, dogth.

Gradgrind Dogs?

Sleary Remarkable animalth.

Gradgrind Yes, their . . . instinct is surprising.

Sleary Exactly, Thquire! Their inthtinct. The dithtanth they'll come to find you.

Pause

Gradgrind Interesting though the subject is , Mr Sleary ...

Sleary Exthactly. Fourteen month ago, Thquire, we were at Chethter, getting up ... Babeth in the Wood, it wath ... when in cometh a dog, in very bad condition, that had obviouthly travelled a long way. He came up to me, Thquire, thtood on hith hind legth, wagged hith tail ... and died on the thpot. Thquire, that dog wath Merrylegth.

Gradgrind Sissy's father's dog!

Sleary Thath it, Thquire. Now I can take my oath from my knowledge of that dog, that the man mutht hath been dead, or Merrylegth would never have left him. Tho. We talked over it for thome time, and decided to do nothing. Why upthet Thethilia? Why unthettle her mind? Perhapth he meant to return. We thhall never know. In any cathe, ith beth to leave thingth ath they are.

Gradgrind She keeps the bottle of nine oils to this very day. And she will believe in his affection till the last moment of her life.

Sleary It theemth to prethent two thingth to a perthon, don't it Thquire? One, that there ith a love in the world, not all thelf-interetht after all, but thomething very different: t'other, that it hath a way of ith own of calculating thath hard to give a name to.

Pause

Well, time to be on my way, Thquire. Thake handth, firtht and latht!

They do

Don't be croth with uth poor vagabondth. People mutht be amuthed. They can't alwayth be a learning, nor yet they can't be alwayth a-working, they aren't made for it. You *mutht* have uth, Thquire. Do the withe thing, and the kind thing too, and make the betht of uth, not the wortht!

He goes

Gradgrind stands, looking off. The Lights cross-fade into a general lighting state

Scene 30

Gradgrind How much of the future did Gradgrind see on the long journey back from Sleary's circus? Did he see himself, an old man, bending his inflexible theories to appointed circumstances; making his facts and figures subservient to Faith, Hope and Charity, and no longer trying to grind that trio in his dusty little mills? And did he catch himself, therefore much despised by his late political associates? These thing were to be.

Bounderby Into how much of the future did Mr Bounderby project himself, as he stood in his empty house? He saw Mrs Sparsit, fighting out a daily fight at the points of all the weapons in the female armoury with the grudging, smarting, peevish, tormenting Lady Scadgers. But did he see more? Did he catch any glimpse of himself making a show to strangers of Bitzer, the rising young man devoted to his master's merits, who had won

Tom's place? Had he any prescience of the day, five years to come, when Josiah Bounderby of Coketown, was to die of a fit in a Coketown street? Probably not. Yet such things were to be.

Louisa Here was Louisa on the next night, watching the fire as in days of yore. She saw broadsides in the street, signed with her father's name, exonerating the late Stephen Blackpool from suspicion and publishing the guilt of his own son, for such things were of the present. But of the future? Did she see a lonely brother, thousands of miles away, contrite, writing to beg her forgiveness? And that same brother's death in a fever hospital in a strange land? Such things were to be.

Sissy Sissy married, her children loving her, beautifying the lives that touched hers with those imaginative graces and delights, without which the heart will wither up. These things were to be.

Louisa Herself again a wife—a mother—lovingly watchful of her children, ever careful that they should have a childhood of the mind, a childhood of the body and a childhood of the imagination. Did Louisa see this? Such a thing was never to be.

Actress 1 (*to the audience*) It rests with you and us, whether in our different fields of action, similar things shall be or not. Let them be! We shall sit with lighter bosoms on the hearth, to see the ashes of our fires turn grey and cold.

Some moments

Black-out

FURNITURE AND PROPERTY

Only basic props and furniture are listed here, most of these being brought on and off by the actors—see Introduction.

SCENE 1

On stage: Wooden benches

SCENE 2

On stage: Nil

SCENE 3

On stage: Chairs
Hearthrug
Needlework for **Mrs Gradgrind**

Personal: **Louisa:** handkerchief

SCENE 4

On stage: Nil

Off stage: Bottle of oil **(Sissy)**
Bundle of clothes **(Emma)**

SCENE 5

On stage: Table. *On it:* teapot, cups, saucers, *etc.*
Chairs

SCENE 6

On stage: Chairs

SCENE 7

On stage: As Scene 6, plus book for **Louisa**

SCENE 8

On stage: Bed
Chair

SCENE 9

On stage: Table. *On it:* lunch dishes
Chairs
Needlework for **Mrs Sparsit**

SCENE 10

On stage: Nil

SCENE 11

On stage: Chairs

SCENE 12

On stage: Chairs
Small table
Piece of cambric, scissors for **Mrs Sparsit**

Off stage: Bottle of smelling salts **(Bounderby)**

SCENE 13

On stage: Platform or chair (*optional*)
Confetti, champagne

Personal: **Tom:** cigar, brandy glass

SCENE 14

On stage: Table
Chair

Off stage: Tea-tray **(Bitzer)**

SCENE 15

On stage: Book for **Harthouse**

SCENE 16

On stage: Chairs
Glasses, bottle of brandy

Personal: **Harthouse:** cigars

SCENE 17

On stage: Chairs

SCENE 18

On stage: As Scene 9

SCENE 19

On stage: As Scene 8

Personal: **Louisa:** purse with banknote and 2 coins

SCENE 20

On stage: Bench

SCENE 21

On stage: As Scene 12, plus:
Book for **Louisa**
Backgammon set

Off stage: Lighted oil-lamp **(Louisa)**

SCENE 22

On stage: Bench in garden

SCENE 23

On stage: Chairs

SCENE 24

On stage: Chairs

Personal: **Waiter:** notebook and pencil

SCENE 25

On stage: Chairs

SCENE 26

On stage: Placard (optional)

SCENE 27

On stage: As Scene 12

SCENE 28

On stage: Nil

Off stage: Long rope, lighted lanterns **(Rescuers)**
Makeshift stretcher **(Rescuers)**

SCENE 29

On stage: As Scene 3

Off stage: Glass of brandy and water **(Sleary)**
Towel **(Tom)**

SCENE 30

On stage: Nil

LIGHTING PLOT

Property fittings required: oil-lamp, lanterns

Various simple interior and exterior settings

PROLOGUE, SCENES 1–19

To open: General lighting downstage

Cue 1	**Actress 2:** "Book the First: Sowing". *Bring up lights on schoolroom*	(Page 2)
Cue 2	The pupils disperse *Lights concentrate around* **Gradgrind**	(Page 3)
Cue 3	Company create Sleary's Horse-Riding Circus *Bright circus lighting*	(Page 4)
Cue 4	**Sleary:** "... Thakespearian quipth and retorth." *Decrease lighting*	(Page 4)
Cue 5	**Gradgrind** leads **Louisa** off *Cross-fade to* **Actor 1**	(Page 4)
Cue 6	Actor 1: "... of its being his birthday." *Bring up lights on drawing-room*	(Page 5)
Cue 7	**Louisa** rubs her face with her handkerchief *Cross-fade to* **Gradgrind**	(Page 7)
Cue 8	**Gradgrind:** "... not quite drunk." *Bring up general lighting—evening*	(Page 7)
Cue 9	**Actress 1** returns *Cross-fade to* **Actress 1**	(Page 10)
Cue 10	**Actress 1:** "... as he took his breakfast." *Bring up lights on Bounderby's dining-room*	(Page 10)
Cue 11	**Mrs Sparsit:** "... of that retreat all evening." *Fade lights around* **Mrs Sparsit**; *bring up lights on* **Actor 2** *and* **Actress 2**	(Page 12)
Cue 12	**Actress 2:** "... began to wonder." *Change to evening lighting (twilight)—fire effect*	(Page 12)
Cue 13	**Louisa:** "... I can hope to do in it." *Pause, then fade lights; bring up lights again at once on* **Sissy**	(Page 14)
Cue 14	**Sissy:** "... but no wiser." *Increase to general lighting*	(Page 14)
Cue 15	**Louisa:** "... with compassion to the door." *Fade lights on* **Louisa**, *then bring up immediately on* **Actor 1**	(Page 15)
Cue 16	As Company create effect of Hands going home from work *Increase to general exterior lighting—evening*	(Page 16)

Cue 17	**Blackpool** goes into his home *Fade to low lighting*	(Page 17)
Cue 18	**Blackpool:** ". . . even in the darkness." *Black-out, then immediately bring up lighting on* **Blackpool**	(Page 17)
Cue 19	**Blackpool:** ". . . so he was admitted." *Change to interior lighting on dining-room*	(Page 17)
Cue 20	**Mrs Sparsit:** ". . . the vices of the people." (*She shakes her head*) *Fade lights on* **Mrs Sparsit** *and* **Bounderby***; bring up lights on* **Blackpool** *in street outside*	(Page 19)
Cue 21	**Actor 1** comes on for Scene 11 *General lighting*	(Page 21)
Cue 22	**Louisa:** ". . . soon subsided into ashes." *Close in lights around* **Louisa**—*fire effect*	(Page 21)
Cue 23	**Tom's voice:** ". . . uncommonly jolly." *Bring up lighting on study*	(Page 23)
Cue 24	**Louisa** goes; **Actor 1** comes on *Cross-fade to* **Actor 1**	(Page 22)
Cue 25	**Actor 1:** ". . . direct from the pantry." *Change to interior evening lighting*—*fire effect*	(Page 26)
Cue 26	**Mrs Sparsit:** ". . . all you desire and deserve." (*She beams at* *him*) *Fade lights, then bring up general lighting on wedding*	(Page 25)
Cue 27	**Louisa** stands, alone. She stares ahead *Fade lights, then bring up lights on* **Actor 2** *and* **Actress 2**	(Page 26)
Cue 28	**Actor 2:** ". . . even in Coketown." *Cross-fade to Mrs Sparsit's apartment*	(Page 27)
Cue 29	**Mrs Sparsit:** ". . . meant the sweetbread." *Fade lights on* **Mrs Sparsit***; bring up lights on library*	(Page 28)
Cue 30	**Tom:** ". . . comply with this request." *Change to hotel room lighting*	(Page 30)
Cue 31	**Actor 2:** ". . . in its filthy waters." *Fade lights; bring up lights on Union Meeting*	(Page 32)
Cue 32	Union Meeting dissolves *Fade to spot on* **Blackpool**	(Page 35)
Cue 33	**Blackpool:** ". . . to see Stephen Blackpool. Now." *Cut spot; bring up lights on Bounderby's dining-room*	(Page 35)
Cue 34	**Bounderby:** "The gold spoon." *Quick black-out; bring up light on* **Blackpool**	(Page 37)
Cue 35	**Blackpool:** ". . . came into the room." *Bring up dim lighting on Blackpool's room*	(Page 37)
Cue 36	**Actor 1:** ". . . to hurry after him." *Or in alternative version:* **Tom:** "Wait for me, Loo!" *Fade to spot on* **Blackpool**	(Page 38 or page 39)
Cue 37	**Blackpool:** ". . . on road out of Coketown." *Slow fade to black-out*	(Page 39)

SCENES 20–30

To open: Spot on **Actress 1**

Cue 38	**Actress 1:** "... would change for him."	(Page 39)
	Increase lighting—hot summer's day	
Cue 39	**Louisa** looks off in **Harthouse's** direction	(Page 42)
	Fade lights; bring up lights on **Actress 2**	
Cue 40	**Actress 2:** "... unexpectedly early hour."	(Page 43)
	Cross-fade to Bounderby's drawing-room	
Cue 41	**Mrs Sparsit:** "Anything will do for me."	(Page 44)
	Fade to spot on **Actress 1**	
Cue 42	**Actress 1:** "... to pity Mr Bounderby."	(Page 44)
	Bring up lights on Bounderby's drawing-room—evening	
Cue 43	**Bounderby** exits	(Page 44)
	Fade lights; increase slightly as **Louisa** *enters with oil-lamp*	
Cue 44	**Tom** bows his head and gives a stifled cry	(Page 45)
	Pause, then fade lights	
Cue 45	When ready for Scene 22	(Page 46)
	Bring up general lighting	
Cue 46	**Actor 1:** "... and whirled away."	(Page 47)
	Dim lights	
Cue 47	**Louisa:** "Waiting for the Coketown train."	(Page 48)
	Lightning	
Cue 48	**Gradgrind:** "Louisa!"	(Page 49)
	Bring up lights on Gradgrind's study	
Cue 49	**Gradgrind** tries to hold **Louisa**, but she falls to the ground	(Page 50)
	Quick black-out	
Cue 50	When ready for Scene 24	(Page 51)
	Bring up lights on Harthouse's hotel room	
Cue 51	**Harthouse:** "Camels and be damned."	(Page 53)
	Quick black-out; then bring up lights on **Actress 1** *and* **Actor 1**	
Cue 52	**Actor 1:** "... her off to Stone Lodge."	(Page 53)
	Bring up lights on Gradgrind's study	
Cue 53	**Bounderby:** "... no more to say. Good-night!"	(Page 56)
	Fade to spot on **Actor 1**	
Cue 54	When ready for Scene 26	(Page 56)
	Bring up exterior lighting—evening	
Cue 55	**Rachael:** "All on you!"	(Page 57)
	Fade lights; then bring up lights on **Actors 1** *and* **2, Actresses 1** *and* **2**	
Cue 56	**Actor 2:** "... into Bounderby's house."	(Page 58)
	Bring up lights on Bounderby's drawing-room	
Cue 57	**Actor 1:** "... Josiah Bounderby of Coketown."	(Page 60)
	Black-out	
Cue 58	**Actress 1:** "... did he not come back?"	(Page 60)
	Bring up faint light on **Blackpool's** *face*	

EFFECTS PLOT

Scenes 1–19

Cue 1   **Blackpool:** ". . . forty years of age."   (Page 16)
Sound tape or live music to create atmosphere (optional)

Scenes 20–30

Cue 1   **Tom** waits for train on platform   (Page 47)
Train comes in

Cue 3   **Harthouse** embraces Louisa   (Page 47)
Rain begins to fall, softly at first, then increasing through scene

Cue 4   **Louisa:** "Waiting for the Coketown train."   (Page 48)
Thunder. Increase rain. Train effects

MADE AND PRINTED IN GREAT BRITAIN BY
LATIMER TREND & COMPANY LTD PLYMOUTH

MADE IN ENGLAND